BONATTI

ON LOTS

Treatise 8.2 of Guido Bonatti's
Book of Astronomy

Translated by Benjamin N. Dykes, Ph.D.

From the 1491 and 1550 Latin Editions

The Cazimi Press
Minneapolis, Minnesota
2010

Published and printed in the United States of America
by the Cazimi Press
621 5th Avenue SE #25, Minneapolis, MN 55414

ISBN-13: 978-1-934586-11-2

PUBLISHER'S NOTE:

This reprint of Treatise 8.2 of Guido Bonatti's *Book of Astronomy* has been excerpted from the out-of-print 1st edition, published in 2007. The text reflects the original pagination, and has not been revised or updated to reflect new translation conventions or citations in more recent translations. The Table of Arabic Terms has been removed (a more recent version can be found at: www.bendykes.com/reviews/study.php).

This translation employs the English word "Part," following traditional English and Latin practice. My current translations use the more appropriate word "Lot."

Dr. Benjamin N. Dykes
The Cazimi Press
May, 2010

TABLE OF CONTENTS

Book Abbreviations:

Abu 'Ali al-Khayyat:	*The Judgments of Nativities*	*JN*
Abū Ma'shar:	*Liber Introductorii Maioris ad Scientiam Iudiciorum Astrorum (Great Introduction to the Knowledge of the Judgments of the Stars)*	*Gr. Intr.*
	On Historical Astrology: the Book of Religions and Dynasties (On the Great Conjunctions)	*OGC*
	The Abbreviation of the Introduction to Astrology	*Abbr.*
	The Flowers of Abū Ma'shar	*Flowers*
Al-Biruni:	*The Book of Instruction in the Elements of the Art of Astrology*	*Instr.*
Māshā'allāh:	*De Receptione (On Reception)*	*OR*
	De Revolutionibus Annorum Mundi (On the Revolutions of the Years of the World)	*De Rev. Ann.*
Pseudo-Ptolemy:	*Centiloquium (Centiloquy)*	*Cent.*
Ptolemy	*Tetrabiblos*	*Tet.*
Sahl ibn Bishr:	*De Electionibus (On Elections)*	*On Elect.*
	De Quaestionibus (On Questions)	*On Quest.*
	Introductorium (Introduction)	*Introduct.*
'Umar al-Tabarī:	*Three Books of Nativities*	*TBN*
Vettius Valens:	*The Anthology*	*Anth.*

Table of Figures

TREATISE 8.2: Which is on the Projection of Parts[1] and Their Significations

Chapter 1: The things which we must consider first in particular revolutions, and it is a chapter related to the entire work

Since, by the grace of God, we have sufficiently treated of these things which came above concerning universal revolutions (even though it was by means of a long discussion, albeit not a tedious one), it is fitting (lest something seem to be missing from a treatment of revolutions), that we expand further on the particulars. And the works of our ancients must be examined by means of particular revolutions, just as they were considered in general ones, for they considered it a very useful and fitting and opportune thing–and this was the extraction of Parts concerning matters which we use in the revolutions of years, and which fall to us (and they occur frequently in the work of astronomy), and from which those willing to can attain to very great usefulness in revolutions.

And Abū Ma'shar said[2] that this happens in two ways. Namely, one [way] when one planet is joined to another, or when it is being separated from it by a perceptible quantity: because then it acquires some signification of good or bad, since the planet signifies something else when it advances [toward it], than it would signify when it is with it, and something else when it recedes and is separated from it. For the planets signify certain things by nature, certain things by accident, certain things according to more, certain things according to less, certain things according to equality. Because if two planets equally have signification over one and the same matter, the stronger (namely he who is stronger by nature or power of dignity) is let loose [to act]. Or if one were diurnal and the other nocturnal, or it were the *al-mubtazz* over that Part, or one

---

[1] *Pars* (pl. *partes*) means a "part, portion, share, role, lot or fate, side, faction, direction." The original Greek *kleros* means a "lot" that is cast (whence we get our English word "lottery"). This was translated in Arabic texts by the equivalent word *sah'm*, an "arrow, portion, share, lot," and its related verb *sah'ma*, "to draw/cast lots, to participate in, to share." One Arab form of divination involved drawing arrows as lots from a sheath. Therefore the Latin *pars* means "what is apportioned" or what one's "share" is. Modern English preserves some of this meaning when we ascribe responsibility by saying "for my part." It does not relate to the procedure of measuring lengths of ecliptical longitude when finding the *location* of a Part. Moreover, I note that Firmicus Maternus himself tends to use the word *pars* to mean a "degree." For these reasons I have decided to retain the term "Part."

[2] See *Gr. Intr.*, VIII.1. Almost all of the material in this Treatise is a paraphrase or elaboration of *Gr. Intr.* VIII. I will give cites for explicit references to Abū Ma'shar (or other authors), or in passages where it seems important.

were signifying the beginning, indeed the other one the end, or in some other way it were stronger or more dignified, it is preferred, just as you see in the extraction of the Part of the Father, which the Sun and Saturn equally signify (because each of them signifies fathers). However, it begins from the Sun in the day, because he is stronger than Saturn in the day, for he signifies clarity and splendor, and rejoices in them; indeed Saturn signifies obscurity and shadowiness, and rejoices in them (which are contraries of the aforesaid). And so may you understand about the other things just as will be discussed in its own time and place.

The extraction of the Parts comes to be in the other way (namely the second one), like if there were two or three significators which signify one matter, and the virtue of one were equal to the virtue of the other; or one were more worthy than the other, or stronger. Abū Ma'shar said[3] there will be a similitude in signification, and for these reasons the extraction of Parts was necessary.[4]

For the extraction of Parts is the knowledge of the longitude which is between two significators who naturally signify one matter; nor would the effect of the Part be known well through two significators unless a third were adduced, namely one who naturally signifies the matter on account of which the Part is extracted. For from two significators naturally signifying a matter, derives a space of longitude which is between them; and that from which [the measurement] is begun is called the first significator of the matter; indeed the second one is called the other. And these two are called "immovable." The one from which begins the projection of the degrees of distance which is between the first natural significators, is called the third significator. And the third is the Lord of the Ascendant[5] or the Lord of another house [domicile?] from which the projection of the degrees of distance begins–which is "movable," just as will be handled below in a fitting place. And therefore it was said, take what there is between the one planet and the other, and add from above the degree of the Ascendant, and project from the Ascendant (or from such a place to such a

---

[3] *Gr. Intr.*, VIII.1. Bonatti is paraphrasing Abū Ma'shar and offering his own elaborations.

[4] In other words, Parts are extracted for two reasons: (a) to signify a matter, constructing the Part using planets that naturally signify the matter; and (b) as devices for making interpretive decisions, when it is difficult to decide what the final word on a matter will be. Most Parts are examples of (a), and some can also be used in predictive techniques. Cases like (b) are rarer, but examples can be found in Tr. 5 (146th Consideration), and in Tr. 6, Bonatti's "secret Part" in questions on the 7th House, Ch. 9.

[5] I am not sure why Bonatti says this. Almost every Part is projected from a house cusp, not from a house's Lord.

place, or from such a planet to such a one), giving 30° by equal degrees to each sign. And where the number comes to an end, there will be the Part.[6]

And this was done in three ways, and for two reasons:[7] of which one [reason] was that it might be known what must be judged about the good or the bad that was signified by the Lord [either] of the sign from the Ascendant in which the Part fell, or from the other place from which the Part was projected. Indeed the second reason was because the Ascendant signifies bodies and the beginnings of all things; however the projection was [sometimes] from planets or other places, because that same house or that same planet could be of the same kind or complexion with the place of the Part.

And Abū Ma'shar said,[8] since the Ascendant and the house of the circle from which the longitude (which is between the two natural significators) is projected, changes in every hour, the third significator is named "movable" by means of its signification. Also, for the Parts they use equal degrees, for the reason that the planets are moved about the axis of the circle of signs, and the Ascendant is considered according to the degree of the circle of signs—indeed the degrees of the circle of signs are equal. And Abū Ma'shar said, therefore one planet is in this sign and this degree, and the Ascendant is this or that degree of some sign. And he said that the whole of the circle of signs is spoken of by equal degrees. And he said, however, the degrees of ascensions are from the degrees of the circle wrapping around the circle of signs, and this moves the circle of the signs and the other circles. And Abū Ma'shar said[9] the ancients of Babylon and Egypt and all the rest used 97 Parts, just as was found in their books.

And there are three ways of projecting the Parts: of which the first is the projection of the seven Parts of the seven planets; indeed the second contains the Parts of the twelve houses; the third contains the Parts of the rest of the matters about which there is no mention or reminder in the twelve houses (which are Parts necessary in certain places, both in revolutions and in nativities). The Parts of the first method are seven; of the second, twelve; of the third, ten. But first we must speak of the Parts of the seven planets.

---

[6] There is an ambiguity in Bonatti's instructions, because he regularly says to add the degrees which have already risen above the degree of the Ascendant (or, later, the degrees through which Saturn has passed). This is purely a counting mechanism. For example, if the interval between the two planets were 70°, and the degree of the Ascendant was at 15° Gemini, adding 70° to the degree of the Ascendant (= 25° Leo) is the same as adding 70° + 15° to 0° Gemini.

[7] Bonatti's text mistakenly reads, "in two ways, and for three reasons." See below.

[8] *Gr. Intr.*, VIII.1.

[9] *Gr. Intr.*, VIII.2.

Chapter 2: On the Parts of the seven planets
and their particular significations, and first on the Part of the Moon, which is called the Part of Fortune

Abū Ma'shar said,[10] know that one Part is not extracted except from two significators naturally signifying the matter on account of which the Part is extracted. For if two planets were to signify one matter naturally, and were to agree in diurnality or in other qualities, the extraction of the Part must begin from the stronger one, following what was said elsewhere about the Sun and Saturn (who are equal in the signification of the father and diurnality)–however, the extraction of the Part of the Father is begun from the Sun, because he is stronger on account of the reason given above. And if they were equal in signification just as was said, and one were diurnal and the other nocturnal, the extraction of the Part is begun in the day from the diurnal one, on account of the day prevailing over the night, and it must be preferred to it. Indeed in the night it is begun from the nocturnal one on account of its equality in the signification with the diurnal one, just as it is in the extraction of the Part of Fortune, which is extracted from the luminaries–and the luminaries (as the ancients said) are of equal strength in [good] fortune.

But because the Sun is the diurnal fortune, it begins from the Sun in the day; and because the Moon is nocturnal, it begins from her in the night. And this Part is set out in advance of, and is preferred to, all other Parts, just like the luminaries are preferred to all other stars; and so this Part darkens [by outshining] all other Parts in the way the luminaries darken [by outshining] all other stars. And likewise the Sun is more splendid than all other stars, and is called the luminary of the day, because through his rising it becomes day; and through his setting he is removed, and it becomes night; and he signifies natural life, and the rest of the things which are said in the chapter on his significations. And the Moon is the luminary and fortune of the night, and the significatrix of bodies, and of all things which are said elsewhere in her own chapter.

---

[10] Based on *Gr. Intr.* VIII.3.

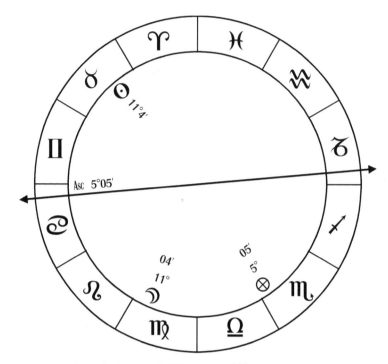

Figure 1: The Part of Fortune

And I will give you an example of the extraction of the Part of Fortune. For let it be put that the Sun is in the twelfth degree and fifth minute of Taurus, and the Moon is in the twelfth degree and fifth minute of Virgo. And let the matter (on account of which you wish to extract the Part of Fortune) be in the day. Thus you must subtract the place of the Sun from the place of the Moon, and there will remain there four signs. And [let there be] 5° and 5' of the ascending sign. And begin to project from the beginning of that same sign by equal degrees, by giving 30° to each sign; and where the number were to end, there will be this Part. And to the contrary in the night–namely you will subtract the place of the Moon from the place of the Sun, and add from above the degrees of the ascending sign, and you will project from the Ascendant, and where the number were to finish, there will be the Part of Fortune. If however both luminaries were in one degree, the Part of Fortune will be in the degree of the Ascendant, and in a like minute.

And this Part signifies life, the body also, and its soul; strength and fortune and substance, and success. Also riches and poverty; even gold and silver; the severity and ease[11] of things bought in the marketplace; even praise and good reputation, and honors and loftiness, good and bad, what is present and what is to be, [whether] hidden or manifest. And it has a signification over every matter; however it does more for the wealthy and for great men than for others. But for every man it also works according to the condition of each one of them.

And if this Part and the luminaries were well disposed in nativities or revolutions, there will be good in a notable way. And it is called the Part of the Moon, and is the Ascendant of the Moon, and signifies good fortune.

And Abū Ma'shar said[12] that when what is absent from the hours of the day in its parts of the hours (that is, of the day), is multiplied, and that from thence was the projection, [then] were it from the place of the Moon by equal degrees, it will fall in the place of [the Part of] Fortune or near the place.

And if one significator were stronger than the other in the place of[13] the Part, the Part will begin from the stronger both in the day and in the night. If however the signification were from the sign and its Lord, this will begin more from the Lord of the sign up to the degrees of the sign, because the signification of the sign is strengthened by the signification of the planet. And if it were to happen that a sign were stronger in the signification, it will begin from the sign, and the Ascendant will be a participant with it (or another place of the circle to which it is extended).[14] And this will be discussed [further] below in the Treatise on revolutions, on the Parts of the twelve houses (and of the things born from earth), more widely and clearly and openly, according to what will happen to each of those Parts when it is treated of them, if God permits.

---

[11] This is a standard phrase Bonatti uses to indicate whether prices and profits are burdensome or not.

[12] This passage is Bonatti's paraphrase of *Gr. Intr.* VIII.3.310-15: "and it was made the Ascendant of the Moon and her Part for this reason, because it is thought that if what she had (out of the hours of the day, in the portions of its hours), were projected after this from the place of the Moon by equal degrees, it would fall onto the place of the Part of Fortune. And we have already proven this, and we have found that perhaps it will have fallen near the place itself." I do not quite understand the instructions, but Abū Ma'shar might be trying to calculate the Part of Fortune during the day, based on what time of day it is.

[13] This word does not quite seem right–if we already knew where the Part fell, we would already have begun from one planet or another.

[14] Bonatti seems to be saying that the point from which Parts are projected is flexible, depending on what the subject matter is, and what its best significator is. But how much the choice is up to us, is not stated. It is also simply true that some Parts are projected from signs and points other than the Ascendant (see below), but this paragraph seems to be implying more.

On the Part of Things to Be, which is called the Part of the Sun[15]

After the Part of Fortune (which exceeds all other Parts in strength and fortune), we must speak next of the Part of Things to Be, which is called the Part of the Sun. And it, immediately after the Part of Fortune, exceeds all other Parts and prevails over them all (even if certain astrologers seem to care very little about it, which to me does not seem fitting, since it is reputed to be a very useful thing by the wise). And this Part is extracted to the contrary of how the Part of Fortune is extracted. For just as the Part of Fortune is extracted in the day from the Sun to the Moon, and in the night from the Moon to the Sun, so the Part of Things to Be is extracted in the day from the Moon to the Sun, and in the night from the Sun to the Moon; and [to this] is added from above what of the ascending sign had ascended; and it is projected from the beginning of the ascending sign, namely by giving 30° to every sign by equal degrees; and where the number were to end, there will be this Part.

For the Parts of the luminaries are set out in advance of the other planets, because even though things to be generated are generated through corruption, and things to be corrupted are corrupted, and corruption comes to be through the motions of the planets, the operations which come to be through the other planets do not appear so openly; nor likewise do those things which come to be by the luminaries, appear like [they do].

And you should know that the peculiar nature of the Part of Things to Be is to signify the soul and body (after the Part of Fortune), and their condition; and faith, and prophecy, religion and the cultivation of God; and secrets, and thoughts, and intentions, and hidden things, and everything that is absent; and courtesy [or courtliness] and liberality [or abundance], and praise, and good reputation, and heat and cold. And Abū Ma'shar said that the significations of the Part of Fortune and the Part of Things to Be appear more regarding every matter both absent and what is going to be, than over what is present. It even reveals more regarding the beginnings of works and over the revolutions of the years (both of the world and of nativities). And he said that the significations of the Part of Fortune appear more in the day than the significations of the Part of Things to Be do, and the significations of the Part of Things to Be appear more in the night than the significations of the Part of Fortune do.[16] And however much mutations and alterations happen by seasons, by the mutation of the

---

[15] In Hellenistic astrology, this is called the Lot of Spirit.

[16] This must mean that the Part of Fortune will have stronger effects with a diurnal *chart* as opposed to a nocturnal one; and the other way around for the Part of Things to Be.

planets from sign to sign, and generations and corruptions come to be, and life comes to be for animals and the rest of the vegetables (and for that reason generated things are deficient and are corrupted)–still, the luminaries operate more openly and perceptibly in them,[17] beyond [what] the other planets [do]. And these two Parts, both for good and evil, operate beyond the rest of the Parts; and their significations are like the significations of the luminaries.

On the Heavy Part, which is called the Part of Saturn[18]

The Part of Saturn,[19] which the wise named the Heavy Part[20] (on account of the grave and heavy things which are signified through it) is taken in the day from Saturn to the Part of Fortune, and in the night the reverse;[21] and it is projected from the Ascendant by giving 30° to every sign, according to equal degrees. And where its number and minutes were to fall, there will be this Part. The significations of which are these: for it signifies memory and profound skill and advice and faith, and religion, and self-control in those things, and con-stancy and durability. And it signifies a matter which had perished or which had gone awry, or which had been stolen or had fled or had been submerged in the sea or in a river, or which had fallen into a pit or a similar place, or had died. And it signifies the condition of the dead, namely by what death a native would die or is going to die. And it signifies the condition of lands and the harvests of others, and things born of the earth; and it especially has inheritances which are purchased. And it signifies heavy buildings, and especially those which are not raised far above the earth; and ditches and accumulations of earth, and the carrying of them on high; and the productions of waters and the like; it even signifies avarice and the hindrance of wretched men living miserably. And it

---

[17] I.e., in natural phenomena. For example, the Sun's effect on the heating and warming of the earth (producing spring and all that goes with it) is much more powerful than the natural effects that, say, Saturn in a given sign will have.

[18] This is the Hermetic Lot of Nemesis.

[19] Bonatti's source for these planetary Parts is *Gr. Intr.*, VIII.3. But his names for them sometimes depart from Abū Ma'shar's.

[20] It should be constructed from the Part of Fortune to Saturn, not the other way around as stated here.

[21] This phrase is traditional in the list of the Hermetic Lots, but is ambiguous. What should be reversed, especially since the Part of Fortune and the Part of Things to Be (or Spirit) are already reversed? Robert Schmidt has offered a solution which seems to be right: the planetary Parts should always be taken from the Part of Things to Be (or Fortune, whichever is meant) to the planet, and *only* the calculation of the Part of Things to Be (or Fortune) should be reversed. These instructions should be understood for all of the remaining planetary Parts.

signifies praise and blame; and it signifies old age and age making to grow old, and every conquered and incarcerated matter, or thing put in prison, and liberation from prison or binding.

On the Part of Jupiter, which is called the Part of Blessedness[22]

The Part of Jupiter, which the philosophers called the Part of Blessedness and Aid, is taken in the day from the Part of Things to Be (which signifies fortune) to Jupiter (who signifies blessedness and aid), and in the night the reverse; and it is projected from the Ascendant. And its signification is over honor and the attainment of matters, victory and aid and blessedness and benignity; also a praiseworthy end of matters, and the seeking of faith and its fitness, and whatever there is concerning its nature, and belief in God, and eagerness for every good work, and the love of it and of justice and of a just judgment between men; and the buildings of orators [or those praying]; and it signifies wisdom and the wise and the loftiness of the wise; also trust and hope and all good things from which men derive enjoyment, and participating in the good toward one another.

On the Part of Mars, which is called the Part of Boldness[23]

The Part of Mars, which is called the Part of Boldness by the ancients, is taken in the day from Mars to the Part of Fortune,[24] and in the night the reverse; and it is projected from the Ascendant. The significations of which are these: because it signifies the disposition of armies, conflicts, and battles, and the honesty and acuity of the mind, and boldness, strength also, anticipation and greatness of heart, with impulse and haste. It even signifies sinful wantonness from heat, and seductions.

On the Part of Venus, which is called the Part of Love and Concord[25]

The Part of Venus, which is called the Part of Love and Concord, is taken in the day from the Part of Fortune to the Part of Things to Be,[26] and in the night

---

[22] This is the Hermetic Lot of Victory.
[23] This is the Hermetic Lot of Courage.
[24] It should be constructed from the Part of Fortune to Mars, not the other way around as stated here.
[25] This is the Hermetic Lot of Eros.
[26] It should be constructed from the Part of Spirit to Venus, not the other way around as stated here.

the reverse; and it is projected from the Ascendant. The significations of which are these: because it signifies enjoyments, desires, and longings in venereal matters and in their cultivation, both licit and illicit; and in those things which venereal people love and in which they delight, and which the mind desires; and marriage and general matters which pertain to the will to have sexual intercourse, and happiness from games and lively things and delights.

On the Part of Mercury, which is called the Part of Poverty and Middling Intellect[27]

The Part of Mercury, which is called the Part of Poverty and of Middling Intellect, is taken in the day from the Part of Things to Be to the Part of Fortune,[28] and in the night the reverse; and it is projected from the Ascendant. And it signifies these: poverty and smallness of talent and intellect, and it even signifies war and fear and hate and contentions and injuries, and anger in the hour of injuries, and enemies. And it even signifies business deals and buying and selling; also thoughts, whether intelligent or crafty; and writings and number and the seeking of astronomy and diverse sciences.

This is the way of extracting the parts of the seven planets, and these things which were said in them are their significations. Whence, if at some time you were to extract some Part regarding one of the aforesaid significations, and you were to project it in some figure, judge on it according to how you saw the conjunction of it or of its Lord with the planets (or their aspects) for good or bad. Nor do I want to bring forward for you the diversity of the opinions of the ancients—because this is the more correct way than our most reverend predecessors observed: Hermes, Vettius [Valens], [and] Abū Ma'shar (who is the flower of the Latins, even though he studied at Athens where study then flourished),[29] and likewise their followers. Indeed other significations of the Parts will be spoken of below after this, in their proper places and in their proper chapters, if God permits.

---

[27] This is the Hermetic Lot of Necessity.

[28] It should be constructed from the Part of Fortune to Mercury, not the other way around (nor with the Part of Things to Be) as stated here.

[29] Again, Bonatti states his belief that Abū Ma'shar was actually a medieval Latin.

Chapter 3: On the significations of the Parts of the twelve houses

Having spoken of the significations of the Parts of the seven planets and about their extraction, we must speak next about the significations of the parts of the twelve houses, and likewise about their extraction. And above were extracted the Parts which in themselves are more useful and more necessary. And while it was noted in the case of every Part, "take from such a planet to such a one, or from such a place to such a one, and project from the Ascendant," I say [now] that you should always add what was left over (between each place), to that which is from the beginning of the sign from which you are projecting,[30] just as was said in the operation of extracting the Part of Fortune, according to how they extracted others.

Nor does it seem to me that differences of opinion are to be recited here, but only to apply the mind to what is the more useful. For the ends of all individual things are not what are signified by every house, but different ones,[31] even if some might have a beginning or origin from the same house, and certain others from others, just like on the things signified by death, the ends of which [significations] will not be the same, but they all signify death. For certain people die from infirmities in their own beds or elsewhere, other from short illnesses, others from long ones; others die from sudden events, others by iron; others by fire; others are suffocated; others drowned; others hanged; and men die in practically innumerable ways. And even though the ways are not the same, still any one of them is death. So it is with the professional responsibilities that are signified by the 10th house: because one is a magistracy, another a kingdom, another a rulership, another a generalship, another the imperial retinue, another some manual profession, and the like. And even though the ways are not the same, still they all have their origin from a matter signifying honor and dignity. And so with any of the things signified by any house, each one according to its own nature, and according to the nature of the house whose signification it was necessary to know.

---

[30] Bonatti's explanation causes unnecessary confusion. He is trying to reiterate the point that, for the sake of convenience in counting, we can add (a) the degrees that have passed from the beginning of the rising sign to the degree of the Ascendant, to (b) the distance between the first two significators, and project the whole amount from the beginning of the rising sign. Again, the result is the same as projecting (b) directly from the degree of the cusp of the Ascendant.

[31] Omitting *eidem*–not sure of its role.

And additional Parts will be found, which it would take a long time to list. You however will consider them just as they will come to your hands through your own industry; nor let what I have told you burden you. And if not all that is signified by the houses can be revealed to you at one and the same time, they will expose some for you, how many and how much that they could suffice for you for the extraction of the Parts of all the houses. Because from that, some honest person would see the Part[32] of the significators of some matter signified by one of the houses of the circle–he could, from his own industry, openly comprehend enough what had not yet been expounded to him.

Chapter 4: On the Parts of the 1st house, that is of the Ascendant,[33] and on their extraction and the things signified by them

Now on extracting the Parts of the twelve houses, and first on the 1st house, namely of the Ascendant and on the significations of its Parts, and their extraction.[34]

The 1st house, as was said above in the chapter on the twelve houses, signifies natural life. And I say "natural" on account of [the fact that] an incident or some accident is often (or rather mostly) the power of nature, just as was said above in another chapter. And therefore from it must be considered the Part of Life and its extraction. For through it is discerned the quality of the life of a native, and of what sort his condition is going to be. And it is extracted from Jupiter and Saturn, on account of their height and far remoteness from the earth, and on account of the fact that their motion is slower than all the rest of the planets. And therefore to them is given virtue over matters whose length [in time] and durability we seek. And because of the reason above, the Ascendant participates with them. And this Part is taken in the day from Jupiter to Saturn, and the reverse in the night; and it is projected from the Ascendant.[35] And this Part is a significatrix of natural life, and signifies the condition of the body and its sustenance. Which if it were well disposed, it signifies the long length of life and its continuation, and the good condition of the body, and the liveliness of

---

[32] Or "role." This sentence is ambiguous–is Bonatti advocating the use of additional Parts for those who are experienced, or he is saying that the use of the Parts he lists will clarify what role significators themselves play in delineating matters?

[33] Or: "On the Parts of the 1st domicile, that is, of the rising one [Ascendant]."

[34] All of the Parts of the houses are found in *Gr. Intr.*, VIII.4.

[35] This is identical to the Part of Children. Note that if the Part of Children is afflicted, it is a sign of not having biological children–which is one way in which a native's biological life will not be extended to future generations.

the soul. If however it were impeded, it signifies a small amount of life and its shortness, and its bad condition with a multitude of diverse infirmities, and with the grief of the soul and its sorrow. It will signify this same thing about the condition of men in revolutions of years, both of the years of the native and of the years of the world.

Having spoken about the first Part of the Ascendant, which is the Part of Life, we must speak next about its second Part, which is the Part of Durability and Stability. And it is the Part of the Security of the Ascendant.[36] For since it[37] is the more noble and more dignified accident that may happen in this world, it was necessary that it be perfected more nobly by durability and stability; and it was necessary that this be by the joining together or complexion of the body and soul; and this was not able to come to be except by the stronger of the supercelestial bodies–and they are the luminaries, whose Parts are found to be stronger and more fortunate than the rest. And so the luminaries are stronger benefics than the other benefics, inasmuch as their effects are sensed more strongly and openly than the rest of the effects [of the planets]. And their Parts signify the body and soul,[38] as do the luminaries themselves signify. Nor can durability come to be or last without the joining together of the body and soul in living things, and so through their complexion or joining they come to be and endure, just as through their dissolution or separation they are corrupted. And this was the reason which moved the ancient sages to the extracting of this Part. And they numbered it from the Part of Fortune (as it were, from the more dignified) in this way: the Part of Durability (which is the Part of the Security of the Ascendant) is taken in the day from the Part of Fortune to the Part of Things to Be, and in the night the reverse,[39] and it is projected from the Ascendant.

---

[36] I follow Zoller in this translation. *Fiducia* usually means "trust" or "confidence," but it can also mean a "security," i.e., something given in the expectation of getting it back. This seems more fitting because (per Bonatti's explanation), living bodies are only temporarily granted a joining of body and soul–when they die, the soul is, so to speak, taken back.

[37] This probably refers to having life, or having a soul joined to a body.

[38] I.e., the Part of Fortune and Part of Things to be (the Part of Spirit), respectively.

[39] Remember that only the calculations of the Parts of Fortune and of Things to be are to be reversed, not the order of their projection. According to Schmidt, this Part is the Hellenistic Lot of *Basis*, which has connotations of firmness and foundation (like our English "basis"). But in Hellenistic doctrine, one takes the shortest distance between them (whether by day or night) and projects it from the Ascendant. This has the result that the Part of *Basis* will always be below the earth, which is fitting for something like a foundation.

And Abū Ma'shar said[40] this Part coincides with the Part of Venus.[41] And certain other things are taken up through this Part which are not taken up through other Parts. And this Part signifies the elegance of the native and likewise his deformity; and his resemblance to his own parents. And if this Part or its Lord were well disposed in someone's nativity, the native will be beautiful in body, beautiful in face, and encompassed everywhere by beauty and health in all parts of his body, and it will be extended to his descendants; and this will last until some malefic stands in their way and impedes them.[42] And he will abound in good things, and the more so if the Part of Fortune and the Part of Things to Be were well disposed; and more again if their Lords were made fortunate–for then he will have from every one what he wishes, and this will be both in journeys or pilgrimages and in other places of much and the greatest seeking. If however this Part were impeded, it signifies the deformity and ugly form of the native, and his body [will be] badly complexioned [or joined together], surrounded by infirmities, and he will be unfortunate, and everything will go to the contrary according to the position and disposition of the aforesaid Part, and of the aforesaid significators. And perhaps this will be extended to his own descendants until some benefic will encounter their significators in some nativity of one of them. And Abū Ma'shar said[43] if it [and its Lord] were to slope towards the significator of the mother, he will be like, and [be] a household member to, his mother.[44]

And he said[45] if you wished to know the durability of some matter, whether it is a nativity or question or revolution, or in any other way you wished to know its durability or defect, whether the matter is known or unknown, whether open or hidden, look at this Part to see if the Lord of the domicile or exaltation or two of the other dignities of the sign in which it is, were to aspect it, or if it were with the Lord of the Ascendant of that year or with one of the Lords of the angles. And were it in an angle, it signifies the stability and durability of the matter (and more greatly so and more firmly, if it is in the 1st or the 10th). If however it were in a cadent, it signifies its removal and destruction. If however it were in a succeedent (and more strongly so if it were in the 2nd or the 8th), it

---

[40] *Gr. Intr.* VIII.4.566.
[41] It is not the same.
[42] I.e., in their nativity–see below.
[43] *Gr. Intr.* VIII.4.575.
[44] Abū Ma'shar (*ibid.*) also says that he will be like his father if it and its Lord "slope towards" (*declinaverint*) the significator of the father.
[45] *Gr. Intr.* VIII.4.579.

signifies the durability of the matter will always be doubtful and fearful. If however it were impeded in an angle, it signifies durability with sorrow and horribleness. But if a benefic were with it, or were to aspect it from a trine or sextile aspect (or even by a square with reception), nor were the benefic impeded, there will be durability in the house, even though with fear or suspicion. And Abū Ma'shar said[46] if it were made fortunate in its own receding, he will find enjoyment by means of the benefic following its receding. If however it were impeded, it will be bad and horrible according to the quantity of its approach [or likeness]. And if it were in some revolution, as was said concerning the Part, it will be in men beyond what it usually is, and they will be more stable and constant and firm than usual.

Having spoken about the first and second Parts of the Ascendant, we must now speak about its third Part, which is called the Part of Reason and Sense. And since one cannot truly be a human without reason and sense, the sages considered whence they could extract a Part of Reason and Sense. And since they saw that Mercury was naturally the significator of each (also of thoughts and speech and thinking), and Mars was the significator of heat and motion, they extracted from these two a Part which they called the Part of Reason and Sense (this can even be called the Part of Thought and Speech)—which is taken in the day from Mercury to Mars, and in the night the reverse; and it is projected from the Ascendant. And they said that this Part signifies sense and reason; and it even signifies knowledge and thought and thinking and speaking. Which if this Part were well disposed in someone's nativity, and it or the Lord of the domicile in which it is, were with the Lord of the Ascendant, or the Lord of the Ascendant were to aspect [the Lord of the Part] in his own dignity,[47] and Mercury were then to aspect the Part and the Lord of the Ascendant or the Lord of the Part by a trine or sextile aspect (or at least from a square with reception), and [Mercury] were made fortunate and strong, nor impeded, the native will be rational, knowledgeable, speaking, thinking, and perceptive. And if Mars were then to aspect the Ascendant or its Lord of the Lord of the Part, the native will be wise, as I said, and he will have an acute mind, easily learning; and

[46] Gr. Intr. VIII.4.588.

[47] Abū Ma'shar (Gr. Intr. VIII.4.599) says: "And if this Part or its Lord were with the Lord of the Ascendant or in the sign in which the Lord of the Ascendant had testimony, and Mercury were to aspect them by a strong aspect..." Bonatti's statement suggests the Lord of the Part ought to be in the domicile of the Lord of the Ascendant's dignity. But Abū Ma'shar's statement suggests the Lord of the Part should be in a sign aspected by the Lord of the Ascendant.

those things which he learned, he will retain well, nor will he be forgetful. And if it were in some revolution [of the years of the world], as was said in nativities, men in that revolution will be of a better mind and better intellect, and better memory than they usually do.

Having spoken of the first, and second, and third Parts of the 1st house, it remains to speak of its fourth Part, which is called the Part of the *Hīlāj*[48]–about which many of the more ancient people did not care to make mention, because it is joined together with others, none of which can exist without it. Indeed without others it can exist well, for it is related to the others like matter to form. And the wise would have been able to set it out if they wanted to, but they set it aside on account of the aforesaid reason. For it is the root of the others, and is taken in the day and night from the degree of the conjunction or prevention which was before the nativity or question or revolution, to the degree of the Moon; and it is projected from the Ascendant. And this Part is called the "root of life" because it comprehends generally the whole nature [or condition] of the native's or querent's life; or even the revolution's. Which if it were well disposed, it signifies the generally good condition of the native's life, and of the other things subject to it. If however it were badly disposed, it signifies the contrary of the aforesaid.

Chapter 5: On the Parts of the 2nd house, and on their extraction and their significations

After it was discussed above concerning the Parts of the 1st house, we must speak immediately about the Parts of the 2nd house, which is called the house of substance, because the first thing a man is in need of after his being born, is substance (and firstly [was] life). And therefore the signification of substance was given to the 2nd house.

Its first Part is called the Part of Substance, which is taken in the day and night from the Lord of the house of substance up to the degree of the house of substance; and it is projected from the Ascendant. And this Part signifies the sustaining of the life of men, and their seeking, and the rest of the things which men use for their sustenance. Which if it were well disposed and well placed, it signifies the good condition of the native and querent, both in sustenance and in wealth and the like. If however it were impeded, it signifies the contrary of the

---

[48] Abū Ma'shar himself groups this Part with the next classification of Parts (*Gr. Intr.*, VIII.5; see below, Ch. 16).

things which were said. And Abū Ma'shar said the other significators of substance and fortune signify the rest of the types of fortune appearing from substance (namely what is hoarded up and watched). The same happens in revolutions. And the Part of Poverty [and Middling Intellect][49] belongs to the Parts of Mercury.

And the Part of Moneylenders is taken in the day and night from Saturn to Mercury; and it is projected from the Ascendant. Which if it were made fortunate and well disposed, it signifies wealth and the increase of substance because of lending on interest and moneylenders. If however it were impeded, and the Lord of substance were impeded, it signifies that the native will lose the majority of his substance because of lending on interest and moneylenders and the like (and likewise a querent). The same thing will happen in revolutions, because the substances of men will be disposed according to the disposition of the aforesaid part.

The Part of Blessedness,[50] which elsewhere is called the Part of Jupiter, and is called the Part of Triumph and Victory, is taken in the day from Saturn to Jupiter, and in the night the reverse; and it is projected from the Ascendant.

The fourth Part of the 2nd house, which is called the Part of Collection, is taken in the day from Mercury to Venus, and in the night the reverse; and it is projected from the Ascendant. And this Part signifies lost things or half-dispersed things, which one sometimes finds in journeys on roads, in camps, on the seashore or banks [of rivers], mountains, or by digging, or other means not named; or if there were a thing which had fallen or fled from someone, or he had forgotten it, or it had gone away from its master in another like manner, or had gone out of his hands. The which Part, if it were in an angle and one of the Lords of some dignity of the sign in which it is (or one of the luminaries) were joined to it (unless it were combust), or he were to aspect it from a trine or sextile aspect, [one] of the aforesaid things will arrive in his hands, and he will be made fortunate in them; and he will find his things if they were to fall from him or he had forgotten them or it had fled from him (as was said regarding strangers [above]). And if the significators of the Part were of good condition in the places in which they were, and in the root of the nativity, the finder or rediscoverer will have good, and success, and usefulness, and fortune from the things which he were to so find. If however the aforesaid significators were badly disposed, it will not work out for him to find it, nor will he gain wealth

---

[49] See above, Ch. 3.
[50] Abū Ma'shar does not re-list this Part here, and anyway the formula differs.

from it, but rather the contrary (and harm) will happen to him. The same will happen to men in revolutions, if the aforesaid Part or the aforesaid significators were so disposed.

Chapter 6: On the Parts of the 3rd house, and on their extraction and their significations

The 3rd house has three Parts. The first is [the Part] of Siblings, and it is taken in the day and night from Saturn to Jupiter; and it is projected from the Ascendant. And the Lord of the domicile of this Part signifies the matter of brothers and their concord. And if this Part falls in a sign of many children, the brothers will be many. And the number of brothers is known by the number which is between this Part and its Lord by the signs, giving one brother to each sign.

The second one, the Part of the Number of Siblings, is taken [by day and night] from Mercury to Saturn; and it is joined, *etc.* and projected from the Ascendant. And if it falls in a sign of many children, the brothers and sisters will be more, according to the number of the signs and planets; and perhaps the number will reach to the quantity of the [lesser] years of the planets, or the middle or greater [years]. And the aspecting planets increase their years. And if this Part falls in a sign of few children, they will be few.

The third is the Part of the Death of Brothers and Sisters. This is taken in the day from the Sun to the degree of the Midheaven [and in the night the reverse], and they are increased and projected from the Ascendant.[51] And it signifies the cause of the death of the brothers and sisters. And when this Part reaches the significators of the brothers and sisters (or *vice versa*) according to profection by sign, and according to direction by degree, the brothers and sisters will have evil.

Chapter 7: On the Parts of the 4th house, and on their extraction and their significations

Now we must discuss the Parts of the 4th house, and first concerning the Part of the Father, which is taken in the day from the Sun to Saturn and in the night the reverse; and it is projected from the Ascendant. And this Part is taken

---

[51] Al-Qabīsī says it is extracted by day from the "Sun to Saturn, by night the opposite, and is cast out from the ascendant. If Saturn is under the rays, take [it] by day from the Sun to Jupiter, by night the opposite, and [it] is cast out from the ascendant" (*Introduction*, V.6).

from these two planets because Saturn signifies agedness and masculinity, and the Sun signifies natural heat, which is the cause of the life of animals; and fathers are more aged than children, and are the cause of children. If however it happened that Saturn was under the rays of the Sun, then the Part of the Father is taken in the day from the Sun to Jupiter, and in the night the reverse; and it is projected from the Ascendant. And Abū Ma'shar said that the Lord of the Part[52] of the Father signifies the fortune of the father, and his substance and labors. Which if the Part were of good condition, the father will be noble. And if its Lord were of good condition, he will be made fortunate and have a long life. If however he were impeded or badly located, he will be laborious, made unfortunate and have a short life. And he said its Lord signifies the kingdom of the native, his honors and strengths.

The second Part of the 4th house, which is called the Part of the Death of the Father, is taken in the day from Saturn to Jupiter, and in the night the reverse; and it is projected from the Ascendant. And this Part signifies the cause of the death of fathers. And however often the profection of the year were to arrive at this Part, or to its Lord, it signifies danger and something horrible for the father; likewise if one of them were to come to the significators of the father.

The third Part of the 4th house, which is called the Part of Grandfathers, is taken in the day from the Lord of the domicile of the Sun to Saturn, and in the night the reverse; and it is projected from the Ascendant. Which if the Sun were in Leo, it is taken in the day from the first degree of Leo to Saturn, and in the night the reverse; and it is projected from the Ascendant. And if [the Sun] were in Capricorn or in Aquarius, it is taken in the day from the Sun to Saturn and in the night the reverse; and it is projected from the Ascendant (nor should you care now whether Saturn is under the rays of the Sun or not). This Part signifies the matters of grandfathers. Whence, whenever it is joined with the benefics, they will discover the good of the grandfather. And however often it were joined to malefics, they will discover the dangers of the grandfather.

The fourth Part of the 4th house, which is called the Part of Relations or of Kindred or of Excellence,[53] is taken in the day from Saturn to Mars and in the night the reverse; and it is projected from the Ascendant. And from above are added the degrees which Mercury[54] had traveled through, of the sign in which he is, and it is projected from the beginning of the same sign; and where it were

---

[52] Reading partis (with Abū Ma'shar, Gr. Intr. VIII.4.719) for domus.
[53] Generositatis. This is meant in the sense of having a noble or excellent family.
[54] Reading Mercurius (with Abū Ma'shar) for Saturnus.

to fall, there will be this Part. And Abū Ma'shar said, after this, look to see if this Part were in an angle and one of the Lords of the dignities of the sign in which it were, were to aspect it–if either the Sun, or the Lord of the 10th, or one of the Lords of the angles, with an aspect of friendship, the native will be of noble progeny or honest relations. If however the Part were cadent from the angles and joined to malefics, or none of the Lords of the dignities of the sign in which it is, or [none] of the Lords of the angles were to aspect it, he will be despised in his relations or kindred or his excellence [or nobility].

The fifth Part of the 4th house, which is called the Part of Inheritances or Possessions [according to Hermes], is taken in the day and night from Saturn to the Moon; and it is projected from the Ascendant. And Abū Ma'shar said[55] that this Part coincides with the Part of the King or the Kingdom, or what kind of work the native will do;[56] which if it were of good condition and well placed, and likewise its Lord, the native will be made fortunate because of inheritances and because of the cultivation of the earth and seeds, and he will acquire substance. Indeed if it were of bad condition and badly placed, it signifies griefs and sorrows and dejections or evil and a horrible thing because of the aforesaid.

Moreover, another Part of Inheritances is had according to the Persian sages, and it is the sixth Part of the 4th house. And this Part is taken in the day from Mercury to Jupiter, and in the night the reverse; and it is projected from the Ascendant. This Part is considered neither in a kingdom nor in the profession, nor in the cultivation of the earth, nor in seeds, but only in matters which are called "hereditary."

The seventh Part of the 4th house, which is called the Part of the Cultivation of the Earth, is taken in the day and night from Venus to Saturn; and it is projected from the Ascendant. Which if it were made fortunate, and its Lord were made fortunate, the native or querent will have something good and useful from the cultivation of the earth, seed, and planting. And he will be made fortunate in them. Likewise this will happen to men generally (from the aforesaid [matters]) in revolutions of years of the world, and to natives in revolutions of nativities, if the aforesaid were so disposed. If however they were impeded, good will not happen to them from the aforesaid, but the contrary will attend them.

The eighth Part of the 4th house, according to al-Qabīsī, which is called the Part of the Nobility of the Native (and of him concerning whom it is doubted

---

[55] In *Abbr.*, VI.20-21.
[56] Also known as the Part of Kings, the eighth Part of the 10th House below.

whether he is the son of the father to whom he is attributed, or of another's) is taken in the day from the degree of the Sun to the degree of his own exaltation, and it is projected from the Ascendant.[57]

The ninth Part of the 4th house, which is called the Part of the End of Matters, is taken in the day [and night] from Saturn to the Lord of the domicile of the conjunction (if it were conjunctional) or to the Lord of the domicile of the prevention (if it were preventional); and it is projected from the Ascendant. And Abū Ma'shar said that if this Part and its Lord were in signs of direct ascension, or they were otherwise made fortunate, the end of the matters of the native or the querent will be [of a] good or praiseworthy nature [condition]. If however they were in crooked signs, or were impeded, their ends will be bad. And if one of them were in a direct sign and the other in a crooked sign, their ends will be intertwined, neither totally good, nor totally bad. And Abū Ma'shar said, after this the matter will revert to what the sign (in which the Lord of the Part is) will signify.

Chapter 8: On the Parts of the 5th house, and on their extraction and their significations

Now we must speak about the Parts of the 5th house, and first about the Part of Children, which is taken in the day from Jupiter to Saturn and by night the reverse; and it is projected from the Ascendant. For through this Part is signified whether the native or querent is going to have children or not. And Abū Ma'shar said[58] that if this Part or its Lord were in a sign of many children, he[59] will have many children. And if it were in a sign of few children, he will have few children. And if it were in a sterile sign, he will not have children. If however this Part were to signify children, and it were made fortunate and were of good condition, the children will live. However if it were impeded, it signifies that they will not live. And he said it even signifies the general condition of the children, and how they will behave toward their parents, and how one will love or hate the other. And he said that what there was in terms of signs between

---

[57] No nocturnal variation is given by Bonatti. Al-Qabīsī (V.7) says it is extracted by day from "the degree of the Sun to the degree of its exaltation, by night from the degree of the Moon to the degree of its exaltation, and is cast out from the ascendant. If the Sun is in the degree of its exaltation by day or the Moon is in the degree of its exaltation by night, the indication belongs to the degree of both of them and the degree of the ascendant."

[58] *Gr. Intr.* VIII.4.807.

[59] Omitting *hic.*

this Part and its Lord is taken, and a child is given to each sign. And he said, if however there were a common sign between them, the number of that same sign is multiplied (because two children will be given to him), where at first [only] one was posited. And he said if there were a planet between them, one child will be counted for him, just as was said above concerning brothers.

The second Part of the 5th house, which signifies the hour in which there should be a child, and the number of children, and whether masculine or feminine, is taken in the day and night from Mars to Jupiter; and it is projected from the Ascendant. And this is because the effecting of children is signified by Jupiter on account of the mixed heat and moisture of [his] nature, and [this is] the cause of growth; and [on account of] the signification of Mars over heat, and on account of his motion and delight and eager desire for natural sexual intercourse (or what comes to be more in men). And since a child cannot come to be except by the sexual intercourse of men and women, and through natural heat and the moisture connected to it, these came to be the reason for the extraction of this Part from them.

And Hermes said[60] if the first Part and the rest of the significators of children were to signify children for a native or querent, that this [second] Part signifies their number; and in addition when Jupiter were to arrive to this Part or its place by body or through a trine or sextile aspect (and more strongly so if it were with reception), wherefore if he were to have sexual intercourse, then it signifies that he will generate a child in that same hour (if, however his age permits).[61] And Abū Ma'shar said if it were in a masculine sign, more of his children will be males; and if it were in a feminine sign, more of his children will be females. And he said, if however the significators were to signify a multitude of children for a native or querent, look at this Part and its Lord, to see in which sign it is: because this signifies that there will be children for him according to the number of the lesser years of the Lord of the Part, or the middle or greater [years]. And he said, perhaps the ones aspecting will increase for him, according to their number of years.

The third Part of the 5th house, which signifies male children, is taken in the day and night from the Moon to Jupiter, and is projected from the Ascendant. (Al-Qabīsī said that it is taken in the day from the Lord of the domicile of the Moon to the Moon, and in the night the reverse; and it is projected from the

---

[60] According to Abū Ma'shar, *Gr. Intr.* VIII.4.833.
[61] Abū Ma'shar (*Gr. Intr.* VIII.4.837) says "it will renew a child for him in that same hour." Is Abū Ma'shar speaking about an election for sexual intercourse?

Ascendant.)[62] And this Part is extracted so, because the Moon signifies youth and the lesser age–which, because it generates,[63] is stronger in generating [children] than old or even mature [age] is. And the operations of nature ought to be more noble in that age, or more powerful, than in others, because of the proximity of the nativity. Moreover, to generate males is more noble than to generate females, because males are agents (indeed females are patients), and action is more noble and dignified than undergoing [something]. And Jupiter is the significator of the effecting of children and creation, and their increase (and especially of males). Therefore the wise numbered this Part from them. Indeed Theophilus [of Edessa] and certain other Persian sages seemed to want to say otherwise.[64] But Abū Ma'shar held the saying of Hermes to be something more authoritative. Likewise they said that this Part aided the fortune of the native in the manner of the Part of Fortune; nor is this impugned by the sages of that time.

The fourth Part of the 5th house, which signifies the condition of daughters (according to al-Qabīsī), is taken in the day and night from the Moon to Venus; and it is projected from the Ascendant.

The fifth Part of the 5th house, through which it is known whether a conceived child is male or female, is taken in the day from the Lord of the domicile of the Moon [to the Moon],[65] and in the night the reverse; and it is projected from the Ascendant. And if it were to fall in a masculine sign, then the one born (or the one about whom it is asked), will be male. If in a feminine sign, it will be female.

Chapter 9: On the Parts of the 6th house, and on their extraction and their significations

The narration of the Parts of the 6th house, and first on the Part of Infirmities and Accidents and Inseparable Defects,[66] which is taken in the day from Saturn to Mars, and in the night the reverse; and it is projected from the Ascendant.

---

[62] Bonatti must have looked at the wrong paragraph in his translation of al-Qabīsī when writing this. Al-Qabīsī's formulation appears below as the fifth Part of the 5th house.

[63] *Quae ex quo generat.*

[64] *Gr. Intr.* VIII.4.854ff. Abū Ma'shar claims that certain Persians took the Part in the day from the Moon to Saturn (and in the night the reverse), while Theophilus took the Part in the day *and* night from the Moon to Saturn.

[65] According to al-Qabīsī.

[66] Al-Qabīsī (V.9) says "chronic disease."

The second Part of the 6th house, which is called the Part of Infirmities both Separable and Inseparable, is taken in the day and night from Mercury to Mars; and it is projected from the Ascendant.

The third Part of the 6th house, which is called the Part of Slaves (according to al-Qabīsī and Theophilus), is taken in the day from Mercury to the Moon and in the night the reverse, and it is projected from the Ascendant. Indeed according to Hermes (whose opinion was held as more authentic by the wise), it is taken in the day and night from Mercury to the Moon, and is projected from the Ascendant.[67] And this, because he and the other sages of those times considered male and female slaves, and often ministers and footmen and legates, to be not very faithful, and quickly changeable, and this to the contrary of their masters (more so than to their usefulness). They attributed all of these and other quick things and those of quick change to these lighter planets. And therefore they extracted this Part from them. Which if it were made fortunate and of a good condition, and likewise its Lord, it signifies the native or querent is going to have good from the aforesaid things signified by the Part. If however they were impeded, it signifies the contrary. And if the Part were of a good condition, and its Lord were impeded, or *vice versa*, it signifies that [at first] he will have good from them, [and] then the contrary will happen to them. And if this Part were in a sign of many children, he will have many male and many female slaves or other servants. And if it were in a sign of few children, he will have few servants. If however it were in a sterile sign, he will care little for them. And the same will happen in revolutions concerning the aforesaid Parts for those who have [slaves]. Theophilus and certain others said that this Part is taken from Mercury to the Part of Fortune [and in the night the reverse]. Abū Ma'shar praised the saying of Hermes more.

The fourth Part of the 6th house, which is called the Part of Captives and the Fettered, is taken in the day from the Lord of the domicile of the Sun to the Sun, and in the night from the Lord of the domicile of the Moon to the Moon; and it is projected from the Ascendant. Which if it were to fall in a good place from the Ascendant, and it were with one of the benefics, the querent or captive will be freed from his capture. But if it were to fall in a malign place, and with malefics, it signifies evil and something horrible for the captive or the one in fetters; and perhaps it signifies the death of the captive (especially if the Lord of the 10th were to aspect). And Abū Ma'shar said, if however the Sun were in his own domicile in the day, or the Moon at night, one of them will be the significa-

---

[67] According to Abū Ma'shar (*Gr. Intr.* VIII.4.916).

tor. And he said after this, look at the one of them which was the significator, to see in what kind of place of the circle it is, and from whom it is being separated or to whom it is joined, and work according to that. You may understand the same in revolutions.

Chapter 10: On the Parts of the 7th house, and on their extraction and on their significations

A discussion on the Parts of the 7th house, and first on the Part of Men's Marriage, which is taken in the day and night from Saturn to Venus; and it is projected from the Ascendant. And Hermes and other sages extracted it from these two planets, because Saturn signifies antiquity and durable things, and marriage ought to be one of the durable things; and Saturn even has a signification over masculinity, and Venus has a signification over femininity. And masculinity ought to precede femininity by the nature of masculinity and action. Which if the Part were of good condition and well disposed, it signifies the marriage to be fit and well fortunate; and that the native or querent will profit; and good will follow from the marriage; and it even signifies that he will contract matrimony with a beautiful and proper woman. If however it were impeded, it signifies that the marriage will be bad and harmful, and that harm will follow from it, and harm and danger and unrest with adversities. You will even see if Jupiter were to arrive at the Part or were to aspect it with a praiseworthy aspect, because then the marriage will be praiseworthy, if it were consummated in that hour. And Abū Ma'shar said if this Part were with the Lord of the sign in which it was, or the Sun and Moon were to aspect it and its Lord with a strong and praiseworthy aspect, it signifies that the native or querent will be joined with one of his family relations. You may understand the same about marriages which are made in revolutions, if the aforesaid Part or its Lord were so disposed as was said.

Abū Ma'shar said the second Part of Men's Marriage, which Vettius [Valens] described, is taken in the day and night from the Sun to Venus,[68] and is projected from the Ascendant.

---

[68] Al-Qabīsī says this second Part (according to Valens) should be by day and night from the Sun to the Moon. But Abū Ma'shar is right–at least according to one of his formulations (see *Anth*. II.38).

The third Part of the 7th house is the Part of the Cleverness and Skill of Men toward Women, and it is similar to the Part of Men's Marriage according to Vettius [Valens].[69]

The fourth Part of the 7th house is the Part of Men's Sexual Intercourse with Women, and it is like Vettius [Valens's] Part of Men's Marriage.[70]

The fifth Part of the 7th house,[71] which is called the Part of Luxury and Men's Fornication, is taken in the day and night from Venus to Saturn; and it is projected from the Ascendant. Which if it were in a good place, the marriage will be praiseworthy, and that the man will seduce the woman he wants.[72] If however it were badly located, the marriage will be blameworthy, nor would he be able to seduce one of them. And Abū Ma'shar said, if however it were in a sign signifying impeded sexual intercourse, the man will be of much sexual intercourse, lascivious, and a fornicator. If however it were made fortunate, he will be a man of much sexual intercourse, and his sexual intercourse will be of the praiseworthy sort. And he said, in the signification of the Part of Licentiousness[73] and of Men's Fornication, if the Lord of the Part of Men's Marriage (which Hermes described) were to fall with Vettius's Part, or the Lord of this Part[74] were aspecting the Part of Men's Marriage,[75] he will fornicate with a women before she is conjoined to him by means of marriage, and the matter will be divulged after he will be a fornicator.

The sixth Part of the 7th house, which is called the Part of Women's Marriage, Hermes said[76] (which is similar to the reason for [the Part] of Men's Marriage), is taken in the day and night from Venus to Saturn; and it is projected from the Ascendant. And Abū Ma'shar said that this Part is identical to the Part of the Cultivation of the Earth.[77] Indeed[78] Vettius [Valens] used to take it in the

---

[69] I.e., from the Sun to Venus (by day and night).

[70] Again, the second Part above.

[71] See *Gr. Intr.* VIII.4.976 and 5.38. There is a discrepancy in the formulas. In VIII.4.976, Abū Ma'shar omits the formula but says it is like Valens's Part of Men's Marriage (the second Part of the 7th House, taken from the Sun to Venus by day and night); he repeats this claim at 5.38. But Bonatti's formula here is identical to *Hermes's* Part of *Women's* Marriage (the sixth Part of the 7th House, below).

[72] Reading *seducet* for *succedet*, here and in the next sentence, in parallel with the discussion of women below.

[73] Above this word was "luxury."

[74] I.e., the Part of Luxury and Men's Fornication.

[75] I do not know which of the two Parts of Men's Marriage he means, since he uses *nuptiae* and *coniugium* interchangeably.

[76] According to *Gr. Intr.* VIII.4.994.

[77] *Ibid.*

day and night from the Moon[79] to Mars, and he projected from the Ascendant.[80] However, Hermes was more authoritative than he. If this Part and its Lord were well disposed and of good condition, they will signify a good women by marriage. Indeed if they were impeded, they will signify griefs and sorrows and afflictions or tribulations which he will find because of marriage, and the woman will be licentious.

Moreover Vettius [Valens] took it[81] in another and better way: for he took it in the day and night from the Moon to Mars, and he projected from the Ascendant. And this method pleased Abū Ma'shar more; and this is the seventh Part.

The eighth Part of the 7th house is called the Part of Women's Skill and Cleverness toward Men. Hermes said that it is like the Part of Women's Marriage.[82]

The ninth Part of the 7th house,[83] which is called the Part of Enjoyment and Delight, is taken in the day and night from Venus to the degree and minute of the 7th house;[84] and it is projected from the Ascendant.

The tenth Part of the 7th house, which is called the Part of Women's Licentiousness and their Shamefulness, Vettius [Valens] said,[85] is like the Part of Women's Marriage, which is taken in the day [and night] from Venus to Saturn and projected from the Ascendant.[86] Which if it were of good condition and well disposed, the woman's own marriage will please her, and she will praise it. Indeed if it were of a bad condition, and badly disposed, her own marriage will displease her, and she will revile it, and she will be saddened and afflicted because of it, and she will support herself with cleverness and deceiving the minds of men.[87] And if this Part were of good condition and well located, or it

---

[78] The rest of this paragraph belongs to the seventh Part immediately following. Bonatti is getting carried away and moving to the seventh Part without announcing it.

[79] Reading *Luna* (with Valens and Abū Ma'shar) for *Sole*.

[80] This is correct (*Anth.* II.38).

[81] The Part of Women's Marriage (*Anth.* II.38).

[82] I.e., the sixth Part above. This is from *Gr. Intr.* VIII.4.1010*ff.*

[83] See al-Qabīsī, V.10.

[84] Again, there is a discrepancy between Bonatti's report and Abū Ma'shar's own words. Abū Ma'shar (*Gr. Intr.* VIII.4.1015, 5.42) says this Part is like Valens's Part of Women's Marriage (the seventh Part above). But Bonatti has given the formula for *Hermes's* Part of Men's and Women's Marriage, the twelfth Part below.

[85] *Gr. Intr.* VIII.4.1017.

[86] Again, a discrepancy. Abū Ma'shar calls this the Part of Conjoining with Women, and says it is like Valens's Part of Women's Marriage (the seventh Part above), but Bonatti gives the formula for *Hermes's* Part of Women's Marriage (the sixth Part above).

[87] *Nitetur in calliditatem & ingenii deceptionem virorum.*

were in signs of cleverness and skill (which are Leo, Sagittarius, Capricorn and Pisces), the woman will seduce the man she wants. Indeed if it were outside of a sign of cleverness and skill, or it were otherwise badly located, she would not be able to seduce any of them.

And in the signification of the Part of Conjoining and Their Sexual Intercourse,[88] if[89] it were impeded in a sign signifying sexual intercourse, she will be a shameful fornicatrix by means of evil licentiousness. Indeed if it were made fortunate in a sign signifying sexual intercourse, she will have much pleasure in sexual intercourse, but of the suitable sort.

And in the signification of the Part of Women's Licentiousness and their Shamefulness, Abū Ma'shar said[90] if the Part of Women's Marriage (which Hermes described) were with this Part (which Vettius [Valens] described), and if the Lord of this Part were with the Part of [Women's] Marriage, she will fornicate with a man, then she will be conjoined [in marriage] to him.

The eleventh Part of the 7th house, which is called the Part of the Woman's Religion and Honesty, is taken in the day and night from the Moon to Venus; and it is projected from the Ascendant. And he said this Part is [the Part] of Daughters, which if it were to fall in a fixed sign, or in the aspect of one of the Lords of the dignities of the sign in which it is, or [the aspect] of a benefic, the woman will be honest and religious, even if she strongly desires sexual intercourse. Indeed if the malefics were to aspect it without reception, and it were in a movable sign, the women will have excessive pleasure in the pursuit of sexual intercourse, giving herself to men and inviting them to sexual intercourse, and for a low price; and she will be in every way a fornicatrix.

The twelfth Part of the 7th house, which is called the Part of Men's and Women's Marriage (according to Hermes), is taken from Venus to the degree and minute of the angle of marriages, that is of the [degree of the] seventh; and it is projected from the Ascendant. Which if it were joined to the benefics, the woman will marry. And good will be spoken regarding her marriage. If however it were of a bad condition or badly located, and joined to malefics, or they were to aspect it without perfect reception, her marriage will be divulged and encounter the disapproval of the clans. Indeed if the Lord of the sign in which the Part is, were in a malign place, and Venus [were] under the rays of the Sun,

---

[88] This is the ninth Part immediately above.
[89] Omitting *et.*
[90] *Gr. Intr.* VIII.4.1033-36.

or impeded by Saturn, the woman will forever be unmarried, and she will lead her life in a shameful way.

The thirteenth Part of the 7th house, which is called [the Part] of the Hour of Marriage, is taken in the day and night from the Sun to the Moon, and is projected from the Ascendant. Which if Jupiter were to aspect it by a praiseworthy aspect, or is joined to it corporally, and they were of good condition, and it were for a man, the man will marry a beautiful and honest and pleasing and desirable woman. And Abū Ma'shar said,[91] however, this Part is used thus because if the nativity of the man were to signify that he will marry, this will be the reason for it. Because one luminary is hot, masculine; the other is moist, feminine. And he said, however, through the conjunction of heat and masculinity with moisture and femininity, generation universally happens in this world; and therefore this Part is named thus.

The fourteenth Part of the 7th house, which is called the Part of Skill and Ease of [Arranging a] Marriage, is taken in the day and night from the Sun to the Moon, and is projected from the degree and minute of Venus. Which if it were to fall in a sign of cleverness and were of good condition, made fortunate and strong, and well disposed, it signifies that it will be perfected for him (who was inclined to marriage) with ease, according to how he had contrived it. If however it were impeded and of a bad condition, his marriage will be with duress and affliction; and he will hardly ever be able to attain what he had intended.

The fifteenth Part of the 7th house, which is called the Part of Fathers-in-Law, is taken in the day and night from Saturn to Venus; and it is projected from the Ascendant. And Abū Ma'shar said[92] that this Part is identical to the Part of Men's Marriage which Hermes considered. Which if it were made fortunate and strong and well disposed, and concordant with the Lord of the domicile in which it is, he will be concordant with and benign to the parents and blood-relatives of his wives more so than to his own. Indeed if it were impeded, he will be an enemy to them.

The sixteenth Part of the 7th house, which is called Part of Contenders and Contentions, is taken in the day from Mars to Jupiter and in the night the reverse; and it is projected from the Ascendant. And Abū Ma'shar said that if this Part were in the Ascendant or with [the Ascendant's] Lord in one of the angles, the native will be given to much contention. Which if it were made

---

[91] *Gr. Intr.* VIII.4.1061ff.
[92] *Gr. Intr.* VIII.4.1079.

unfortunate,[93] horrible evil will follow from the contention; but if this Part were to fall with the Lord of the 7th in the Ascendant, he will be of those who contend in person before kings and judges.

Chapter 11: On the Parts of the 8th house, and on their extraction and their significations

In this chapter we must speak about the Parts of the 8th house, and there are five Parts. And first concerning the Part of Death, which is extracted from three significators. For it is taken in the day and night from the Moon to the degree of the 8th house, and from above will be added what Saturn had traveled through (of the sign in which he is), and it is projected from the beginning of the same sign.[94] And it is extracted so, because the Moon is the significatrix of bodies, and the 8th house is the significatrix of death, which destroys bodies, and Saturn has signification over the end of matters, and over grief and sorrow, and beating the breast, and lamentation and distress, and dissolution and destruction (which all follow from death). For this reason signification was given to these three significators over the fact of death. Which if this Part and its Lord were free and of good condition, and well disposed or placed, the native will die in his own bed by a natural death. If however they were impeded, and the benefics (or at least one of them) did not aspect them, the native will die a shameful [or ugly] death. Which if the aforesaid significators were badly disposed (as was said) in some revolution, many will die such a death in that revolution.

The second Part of the 8th house, which is called the Part of the Killing Planet, is taken in the day from the Lord of the Ascendant to the Moon, and in the night the reverse; and it is projected from the Ascendant. This Part is extracted in this way because the Lord of the Ascendant signifies the soul, and the Moon the body (even though sometimes one is put for the other).[95] While

---

[93] Reading *infortunata* (with Abū Ma'shar) for *fortunata*.

[94] Like Bonatti's arithmetical convention of adding the degrees of the rising sign that have already ascended, this instruction is equivalent to saying: take the distance between the Moon and the degree of the 8th house, and project from Saturn. This is identical to al-Qabīsī's account (V.11). I note that in Lemay's critical edition of John of Spain's translation of Abū Ma'shar (*Gr. Intr.* VIII.4.1100), he adds "Lord" in parentheses as a correction, so that it reads: "it is taken in the day and night from the degree of the Moon to the degree of (the Lord of) the eighth house…" For our purposes we should follow al-Qabīsī and Abū Ma'shar's *Abbr.*, but using the Lord of the 8th is an interesting variation that may be worth investigating.

[95] I believe Bonatti means that some people attribute the body to the Lord of the Ascendant and the soul to the Moon.

the soul embraces the body it signifies the temperament [or their mixture]; and they persist while they are united; however when they are divided, the body dies then, even though the soul remains. And therefore the Part was extracted thusly by the sages. And Abū Ma'shar said[96] that if the Moon alone were to aspect the Part, and she (or the Lord of the sign in which the Part is) were in a sign of severed limbs, impeded, or the Lords of the signs in which they are were to impede each other, he will die by suffering. If however they were not impeded, nor did they impede each other, he will be mutilated according to the member deputed to the sign in which the Moon was, but he will not die from that.

The third Part of the 8th house, which is called the Part of the Year in which Death is Feared for the Native (or his affliction or destruction, or impediment or heavy oppression), is taken in the day [and night][97] from Saturn to the Lord of the domicile of the conjunction or prevention which was before the nativity or the question or revolution;[98] and it is projected from the Ascendant. And this Part is extracted thus, because Saturn is the significator or cold and death, and the end, and affliction (which make for destruction); and likewise the degree of the conjunction or prevention.[99] Therefore they numbered the Part from those two places. And Abū Ma'shar said[100] this Part agrees with the Part of the End of Matters. And he said if this Part and its Lord were with the Lord of the Ascendant, [and] impeded, the native will have many infirmities and afflictions in his body and substance, and will often come close to losing his body and the loss of substance. And whenever the year were to arrive at this Part, [or] the Part were to arrive by profections (through which one sign is given to every year) or through a direction (which is by degrees of ascensions) to the Ascendant or its Lord, the native will find dangers in his body and limbs from infirmities; and he will find distress and horrible things in substance; he will also fear death from diverse sources.

The fourth Part of the 8th house, which is called the Part of the Heavy Place, is taken in the day from Saturn to Mars, and in the night the reverse, and from above is added what Mercury had traveled through of the sign in which he is,

---

[96] *Gr. Intr.* VIII.4.1120*ff.*

[97] Following *Gr. Intr.* VIII.4.1132.

[98] Bonatti (or his source) does not report what one should do if Saturn himself is the Lord of the conjunction or prevention–as is reported for similar situations in other Parts.

[99] This is not usually how the degree is described. But the degree of the syzygy is supposed to give information on the quality and end of a nativity, question, or election (see especially Tr. 7).

[100] *Gr. Intr.* VIII.4.1136.

The second Part of the 10th house, which is called the Part of a Kingdom, is taken in the day from Mars to the Moon and in the night the reverse; and it is projected from the Ascendant. And Abū Ma'shar said[111] if this Part and its Lord were of good condition, and they were mixed with the Lord of the 10th and that of the Ascendant, the native will be a king or duke, and will be with wealthy people who will receive his words and will listen to them.[112]

The third Part of the 10th house is called the Part of a Kingdom and Kings and Dispositors. And it is taken in the day from Mercury to Mars, and in the night the reverse; and it is projected from the Ascendant. And this Part was extracted from them because the signification of giving, taking, writing, prohibiting matters, pursuing consulships, of reading letters, sending and receiving orders, and counting monies, and the discernment of skill, is given to Mercury. And the signification of fear and terror is given to Mars. Therefore this Part was numbered from them. Which if it and its Lord were well disposed and of good condition, and well located with the Lord of the Ascendant, the native will be of good character [or skill], teachable and capable of reason, and a consulship will happen to him (if he were fit for that); and he will be a scribe of kings or a tax-collector, or the custodian of their *census* or of the substances of greater kings. And if he were fit for a kingdom or empire, he will attain it, and the reputation of his status will pass on high and be extended up to the ends of the lands, and he will raise up certain men, and exalt them beyond measure–and depose certain powerful people and press them down; and [his] soldiers will run to and fro, and the matters of men will run through his hands.

The fourth Part of the 10th house, which is called the Part of a Kingdom and Victory and Aid, is taken in the day from the Sun to Saturn, and in the night the reverse; and it is projected from the Ascendant. And Abū Ma'shar said[113] this Part is identical to the Part of the Father[114] if Saturn is not[115] under the rays of the Sun. Which if it were well disposed and of good condition, and especially with the Lord of the 10th house, and with the Lord of the Ascendant, it signifies a kingdom for the native (if he were of those who are fit for a kingdom); it even signifies honor and exaltation for each person according to his [social] condi-

---

[111] *Gr. Intr.* VIII.4.1271-73.

[112] This is similar to the Part of the Kingdom and Empire in Ch. 19, except that in Ch. 19 the distance is projected from the degree of the Ascendant of a conjunction which signifies a regime change–perhaps because Mars and the Moon signify things that change and come to an end: see Tr. 4, Ch. 2.

[113] *Gr. Intr.* VIII.4.1291*ff.*

[114] Reading *patris* for *partum*.

[115] Zoller's translation omits "not."

tion, and he will be extended beyond, and preferred to, and prevail over those of his own kind. Abū Ma'shar said[116] if it were in a sign in which the Lord of the Ascendant or the Lord of the 10th had a dignity, it signifies victory for the native over whose who contend with him; the same will happen in revolutions, if this Part were so disposed.

The fifth part of the 10th house, which is called the Part of Those Suddenly Made Lofty, is taken in the day from Saturn to the Part of Fortune, and in the night the reverse; and it is projected from the Ascendant. And Abū Ma'shar said[117] this Part is like the Part of Saturn.[118] Which if it were in some optimal place from the Ascendant and from the benefics in someone's nativity or question, he will suddenly be made lofty. And if the Lord of the Ascendant were with it, or were to aspect it by an aspect of friendship and from a praiseworthy place, and [the Lord] were well disposed, his loftiness will be increased unexpectedly; and he will attain a kingdom most quickly, and in the shortest time, so that men will marvel at it. And Abū Ma'shar said,[119] however, you will look at this Part if you knew that the man will be made lofty, and will acquire a kingdom and honor.[120] And he said, indeed if this Part were impeded, the native or querent will suddenly find evil and impediment and a horrible thing and depression. You may understand the same in revolutions, because if the Part were of good condition and well disposed, the native and others will suddenly acquire good in that revolution; and if it were impeded, they will likewise be impeded.

The sixth Part of the 10th house, which is called the Part of Nobles (and of those who are noted among men, or of honored people) is taken in the day and night from Mercury to the Sun; and it is projected from the Ascendant. Which if it and its Lord were of good condition and well disposed, the native will be noble and honored among kings and nobles and the wealthy and great men. And Abū Ma'shar said[121] if it were with a planet who had great dignity in the Midheaven, he will have a chief position by which he will be celebrated in the manner that a division of the people of a city is celebrated among its own

---

[116] *Gr. Intr.* VIII.4.1296-97.

[117] *Gr. Intr.* VIII.4.1301.

[118] But remember that the true Part of Saturn (or Lot of Nemesis) is constructed from the Part of Fortune to Saturn, and only the calculation of the Part of Fortune is reversed at night.

[119] *Gr. Intr.* VIII.4.1305*ff.*

[120] In other words, a Part cannot be looked at in isolation; the natal figure by itself must show signs of success before the qualification of "sudden" loftiness can be applied.

[121] *Gr. Intr.* VIII.4.1314*ff.*

citizens. If however it were to the contrary, the contrary will happen. You may understand the same in revolutions.

The seventh Part of the 10th house, which is called the Part of Soldiers and Ministers (said Abū Ma'shar),[122] is taken in the day from Mars to Saturn, and in the night the reverse; and it is projected from the Ascendant. And he said, if this Part and its Lord were commingled with the Lord of the Ascendant, the native will follow a king, or he will be from among his soldiers or ministers.

The eighth Part of the 10th house, which is called the Part of Kings (and what a native might do by means of works), is taken in the day and night from Saturn to the Moon; and it is projected from the Ascendant. And this, because Saturn signifies labor, adversity, necessity, poverty, and generally laborious works, like the superintending of houses, ditches, the operations of iron and its extraction from minerals, and other hateful and tedious works, since he is the significator of labor and affliction. And he is the significator of the wealthy whose riches are burdensome and heavy. And the Moon signifies labors and quickness in matters on account of the speed of her motion, and she is the significatrix of the common people–for which reason the wise numbered this Part from them. And Abū Ma'shar said[123] this Part signifies a kingdom and honor and magnificence;[124] and what kind of work the native will do which he might do for its own sake, and what mastery he will exercise; and whether he will acquire [wealth] from his mastery or kingdom, or not. And he said if it were in Gemini or in Virgo, or in the signs of the arts or professions, he will be made lofty through the works of this hands which are necessary for the wealthy (by which they are adorned); and he will be with wealthy and great people because of his experience and skill. And if the Part were commingled by the significators of substance, he will acquire a great quantity of substance from his profession. And he said if it were to the contrary, he will be a pauper in his profession, and unfortunate; he will hardly acquire his daily bread; however he will not be able to be weary, and if he were to be wearied, he will die of starvation. For there will not be anyone who will offer him something to eat. You may understand the same in revolutions, for sometimes there are years in which the fortunate do not earn money–and that is when this Part is badly disposed in the revolution. And sometimes there are years in which the unforunate will earn something–and this is when the Part is well disposed.

---

[122] *Gr. Intr.* VIII.4.1320.

[123] *Gr. Intr.* VIII.4.1334*ff.*

[124] "Magnificence" refers to a traditional Aristotelian virtue involving spending money on great works (which thereby bring fame and honor).

The ninth Part of the 10th house, which is called the Part of Businessmen and Those Working with Their Hands, is taken in the day from Mercury to Venus, and in the night the reverse; and it is projected from the Ascendant. And Abū Ma'shar said[125] this Part is like the Part of Collection. This Part signifies talented men and artisans in their professions, namely in Venereal and Mercurial ones, like knowing how to work gold, silver, precious stones, and the like; and those who know how to do business, namely the buying and selling of this sort of precious and select merchandise, like pearls, rings, and the like; and those who know how to make beautiful vestments and how to adorn them (and especially those which pertain to women); and how to paint and write and make coins and carve sigils and like things which pertain to the nature of Mercury and Venus. Which if this Part and its Lord were of good condition, and well disposed, and were commingled with the Lord of the Ascendant by a conjunction or trine or sextile aspect, the native or querent will be made lofty by the works and business transactions of his own hands: for he will make beautiful instruments by them, and beautiful works which become noble and wealthy and great men. If however it were the contrary, he will not get involved with them because the contrary will happen to him. Because if this Part and its Lord were well disposed in some revolution, both of nativities and of the world, the aforesaid producers will earn wealth from the aforesaid business transaction. However if it were the contrary, the contrary will happen.

The tenth part of the 10th house, which is called the Part of the Business of Buying and Selling, is taken in the day from the Part of Things to Be to the Part of Fortune, and in the night the reverse; and it is projected from the Ascendant.[126] And Abū Ma'shar said this Part is like the Part of Mercury.[127] And he said these Parts[128] (which belong to business transactions), if they are received in the aspects of Mercury, [signify that] the native will be experienced in business matters; and he will have the knowledge of buying and selling; which if they were made fortunate, and well disposed, they will be successful for him, and he will earn money from them and because of them. If however it were of bad condition, and badly disposed, even though he might know [how to engage in

---

[125] *Gr. Intr.* VIII.4.1350.

[126] Again, this should probably only involve reversing their respective calculations at night, so that we are always measuring from the Part of Things to Be to the Part of Fortune.

[127] *Gr. Intr.* VIII.4.1364. Remember that the true Part of Mercury is taken from the Part of Fortune to Mercury, with only the Part of Fortune's calculation being reversed at night, not the order in which they are taken (see Ch. 2).

[128] This Part and the previous Part.

them], he will not get involved in them because it will be to the contrary for him. The same must be understood in revolutions, both of the world and nativities.

The eleventh Part of the 10th house, which is called the Part of Work (and of a matter which it is necessary that it come to be wholly), is taken in the day from the Sun to Jupiter, and in the night the reverse, and it is projected from the Ascendant. And Abū Ma'shar said[129] that this Part is like the Part of Fathers if Saturn were under the rays. And he said if this Part were with the Lord of the Ascendant, the native will be distinguished in his works, because he will know them better than others do, and he will pant and be distressed in every matter which he wants to do and which he hopes to finish quickly; and he will always fear it will not be perfected until he sees it completed. Whence if someone wanted to do something, and wanted to know what was going to be from it, look at this Part: which if it were of good condition (and especially if it were with the benefics), it will profit him if he were to do it, and especially if he were to hurry up and do it. If however it were with the malefics or otherwise impeded, he will find evil and detriment and something horrible if he were to do it because of [hurrying], and by how much more he were to hurry to do it, by that much more worse and horrible will it happen to him from it. And this holds good not only in nativities, it holds true even in questions and revolutions, both of the world and of nativities.

The twelfth Part of the 10th house, which is called the Part of Mothers, is taken in the day from Venus to the Moon, and in the night the reverse; and is projected from the Ascendant. And this Part signifies the condition of mothers. Which if it were of good condition and well disposed, it signifies the good condition of mothers. And if it were in a nativity, in the aspect of the Lord of the Ascendant by a trine or sextile, it signifies the mother will love the son. And if the Lord of the 10th were to receive [the Lord of the Ascendant], namely so the Lord of the Ascendant did not receive the Lord of the 10th or the Moon, it signifies that the mother will love the son; he however will not love the mother. And if the Lord of the Ascendant were to receive the Lord of the 10th, nor [the Lord of the 10th] [the Lord of the Ascendant] nor the Moon, it signifies that the son will love the mother more than she him. If both of them were to receive each other, they both will love each other. If neither were to receive the other, neither will love the other. The same is to be said in questions and revolutions

---

[129] *Gr. Intr.* VIII.4.1373.

and in nativities. And the sages put the Part of the Mother in the 10th because it is opposite the 4th (which signifies the father).

The thirteenth Part of the 10th house, which is called the Part Signifying Whether There is a Reason for a Kingdom or Not, is taken in the day and night from the Sun to the degree of the Midheaven; and it is projected from the degree of Jupiter.[130]

The fourteenth Part of the 10th house, which is called the Part of the Death of the Mother, is taken in the day from Venus to Saturn and in the night the reverse, and it is projected from the Ascendant.[131]

Chapter 14: On the Parts of the 11th house, and on their extraction and their significations

In this chapter we must speak about the Parts of the 11th house, and first about the Part of Excellence and Nobility. Abū Ma'shar said[132] that it is taken in the day from the Part of Fortune to the Part of Things to Be,[133] and in the night the reverse; and it is projected from the Ascendant. And he said that this Part is like the Part of Stability and Durability and the Part of Venus.[134] And this Part was so extracted, because since [the Part] is noble and stable and very useful, it was necessary that it be extracted from two other more noble and excellent Parts, which are the Part of Fortune and the Part of Things to Be. Which if it were of good condition and well disposed, and were well located with benefics (and better if it were in the 10th or 11th, nor did one of the malefics impede it), the native will excel beyond other men, and will be noble and fortunate, and his fortune will last, and he will be praiseworthy and of good condition. And Abū Ma'shar said[135] he will be of those whom men need on account of his fortune, and whom men will revere, and he will be practically a prince among the mass of people. And he said his name will remain through an age of many years, and from every work which he does he will see good and joy, and that it will please him. If however it were to the contrary, the contrary will happen to him. You

---

[130] Al-Qabīsī, V.13.
[131] Source unknown.
[132] *Gr. Intr.* VIII.4.1393*ff.*
[133] If this Part is supposed to be like the Hermetic Part of *Basis* (see above), we should take the *shortest* distance between them, reversing only their respective calculations at night.
[134] Remember that the true Part of Venus is calculated from the Part of Things to Be (or Part of Spirit) to Venus, with only the former's calculation being reversed at night, not the order in which they are taken.
[135] *Gr. Intr.* VIII.4.1399*ff.*

may understand the same in general questions, and it can play a role even in others; and likewise in revolutions. And if this Part were so disposed, good or the contrary will happen to every one according to his condition.

The second Part of the 11th house, which is called the Part Signifying How the Native (or Querent) Will be Loved by Men (or how they will hate him), Abū Ma'shar said,[136] is taken in the day from the Part of Fortune to the Part of Things to Be, and in the night the reverse, and it is projected from the Ascendant.[137] And he said this Part is like the Part of Venus.[138] Which if this Part were to fall in the domicile or exaltation or triplicity of some benefic, and the benefic were to aspect the Part, nor were it impeded by one of the malefics, he will be loved by men and be lovable to them, and sweet and pleasing in their eyes. Indeed if it were to fall with malefics or in their bad aspects, he will be hateful and ponderous among men, nor will they really want to look at him; and often, whatever he does or says will displease men, even when saying and doing good.

The third Part of the 11th house, which is called the Part of One Known[139] among Men and One Honored Among Them (and through whom their matters and business dealings are perfected), is taken in the day from the Part of Fortune to the Sun, and in the night the reverse; and it is projected from the Ascendant. Which if it were well located, namely received by the Sun, Jupiter, or Venus, Mercury and the Moon, with them being benefic,[140] or they were to aspect it and the Lord of the Ascendant by a trine or sextile aspect, the native or querent will be honored both by great men and the common people, and they will love him, and will run back to him for their affairs, and will give him many things in his hands, and many business dealings to perfect or make a determination on, and they will confide very much in him.

The fourth Part of the 11th house, which is called the Part of Luckiness and Profit, is taken in the day from the Part of Fortune to Jupiter, and in the night the reverse; and it is projected from the Ascendant. Which if it were with the Lord of the Ascendant, or he were to aspect it by a trine or sextile aspect (or at least by a square with reception), nor were it otherwise impeded, it signifies that the native will be lucky and make profit [or progress] in all matters, and he will

---

[136] *Gr. Intr.* VIII.4.1407*ff*.

[137] Again, this formulation may be an error.

[138] See the reminder above about the true Part of Venus.

[139] Reading *noti* (with Abū Ma'shar) for *nati*.

[140] *Existentibus fortunis*. Abū Ma'shar says, "Which if this Part were received with the Sun and Jupiter and *the rest of the benefics*" (emphasis mine). I take Bonatti's use of *existo* and the ablative absolute to mean that he wants these good planets to be in a good condition, as well–it is not just a restatement of Abū Ma'shar.

attain the generality of things which are necessary for him (of temporal things), and not only will his matters be perfected, but even the matters of others through his hands, according to how he wants it. Which if, in addition, the benefics were to aspect it, he will attain whatever he might want with ease, so that practically nothing will seem to be lacking from what he wants. And Abū Ma'shar said[141] perhaps that he will acquire something more than what he wants, easily. Indeed if it were not with the Lord of the Ascendant, nor did he aspect it, and the malefics were to aspect it, it will be to the contrary. The same will happen in questions and in revolutions.

The fifth Part of the 11th house, which is called the Part of Coveting (and of the inclination to or the appetite for the love of the world and temporal things), is taken in the day from the Part of Fortune to the Part of Things to Be, and in the night the reverse; and it is projected from the Ascendant.[142] And Abū Ma'shar said[143] this Part is like the Part of Venus.[144] Which if it were in an optimal place in the nativity or question or revolution, he will conquer all his own strong desires and longings. And he said, indeed if it were in a bad place, his own strong desires will conquer him; and he will be inclined toward and have an appetite for the world and its delight, and will lose whatever he had in it.

The sixth Part of the 11th house, which is called the Part of Trust and Hope, is taken in the day from Saturn to Venus, and in the night the reverse; and it is projected from the Ascendant. Which if it were in someone's nativity or question, with it and its Lord in an optimal place, made fortunate[145] (and namely strong), the native or querent will attain everything which he hopes for, and in which he were to have trust. If however they were of poor condition and badly located, he will not attain from it what he hoped, [i.e.,] that it would profit him in a perceptible way. The same will happen in revolutions. For if they were of good condition and well located, men will attain enough of those things for which they wished in that revolution. If however they were impeded, [it will be] to the contrary.

---

[141] *Gr. Intr.* VIII.4.1435-36.

[142] One has to wonder why in particular this same Part is listed under so many houses. Surely it cannot mean both success generally and every individual type of success as well?

[143] *Gr. Intr.* VIII.4.1442-43.

[144] See above.

[145] Reading *fortunata* (with Abū Ma'shar, indicating the Part) for *fortunato* (with Bonatti, indicating the place).

The seventh Part of the 11th house, which is called the Part of Friends, is taken in the day and night from the Moon to Mercury; and it is projected from the Ascendant. And this Part is taken so, because Mercury is a shape-shifter of many diverse things–namely of significations. For at certain times he signifies masculinity, at certain ones femininity; and at certain ones speed, at certain ones slowness; at certain ones heat, at certain ones cold; at certain ones fortune, at certain ones misfortune; and he is always inclined to the nature of the one to which he is joined. Likewise the Moon does the same thing on account of her fast motion and being quickly changeable. Whence, since the wills of men are changed quickly with their friends, nor do they remain long in the same nature, therefore the wise extracted the Part of Friends from those two planets, because they are quicker and more changeable than the rest.[146] Which if the Part were of good condition and well disposed, and its Lord were well disposed and in movable signs, the native or querent will have many friends. Because if they were made fortunate, friends will be useful to him, and he to them, and they will derive enjoyment out of good things with each other. And if they were received, he will be praiseworthy among them and be loved by them. Indeed if it were to the contrary, you will judge the contrary.

The eighth Part of the 11th house, which is called the Part of the Agreement of Friends, (and even of a husband and wife), and their discord, is taken in the day and night from the Part of Things to Be to Mercury; and it is projected from the Ascendant. This Part is of the more difficult ones to comprehend which there are among the Parts, because it is necessary to know the nativity of the native and of those who are posited as his friends (or of a husband and wife). And see[147] if the Part were to fall in the Ascendant of the nativity of the native or with its Lord, without the impediment of the malefics, or if it were in a sign which was the Ascendant of their nativity; or if it were in the 11th or joined with its Lord; or joined with the Lord of the Ascendant, with [the Lord] located in good condition and well disposed, and in the aspect of the benefics, and in a good place from the Ascendant, nor impeded by one of the malefics; or if [the Part] were in the exaltation of one of the planets; or, as Abū Ma'shar said,[148] if it

---

[146] In Aristotelian terms, this sort of fair-weather friendship refers to friendships based on pleasure or usefulness–not deeper friendship based on character. This point should be kept in mind when understanding this Part.

[147] Bonatti seems to be say that we are ought to compare the degree of the Part in one chart with the configuration of planets in the other–as in synastry.

[148] *Gr. Intr.* VIII.4.1480.

were in signs agreeing [with one another].[149] Because if it were so, they will love each other with their friends, and [a husband] with his wife. But if it were in a sign of the descension of one of them, or in the sign of his fall, or in the opposition of the Ascendant, or in signs that are contrary, they will be enemies to one another.

The ninth Part of the 11th house, which is called the Part of Fertility and the Abundance of Good in the Home, is taken in the day and night from the Moon to Mercury, and it is projected from the Ascendant. And Abū Ma'shar said[150] this Part is like the Part of Friends. And he said if it and its Lord were in a good mixture[151] with the Part of Fortune and the Lord of the Ascendant, the native or querent will be plentiful in the home, with all fertility; and if it were otherwise, it will be the contrary. Which if it were so disposed in a revolution, the same will happen.

The tenth Part of the 11th house, which is called the Part of the Honesty of the Mind, is taken in the day from Mercury to the Sun, and in the night the reverse; and it is projected from the Ascendant. Which if it were to fall in a good place with one of the benefics (and especially with Jupiter), or Jupiter or the Sun were to aspect it by a trine or sextile aspect, the native or querent will have a sweet and easy and patient mind. And Abū Ma'shar said[152] if this Part and its Lord were to fall in signs of honesty, he will have an honest mind; and if it were to fall with the malefics or in signs contrary to honesty, it will be to the contrary. You may understand the same in revolutions.

The eleventh Part of the 11th house, which is called the Part of Praise and Gratitude, is taken in the day from Jupiter to Venus, and in the night the reverse; and it is projected from the Ascendant. Whence if it and its Lord were of good condition, and well disposed, and the benefics (and especially Jupiter) were to aspect them or were conjoined to them, the native or querent will be praiseworthy, thanked for every thing to which he is put; and he will be praised for his works, and he will receive benefaction from that. If however they were badly disposed or the malefics were to aspect them, he will not be praised for his works, nor for his services, and by no means will he be praised or receive

---

[149] I believe this means we ought to look at the location of the Part in each native's chart, and compare the signs involved.

[150] *Gr. Intr.* VIII.4.1487.

[151] *Complexione. Complexio* usually refers to innate qualities, but here and above Bonatti *seems* to use it as a synonym for being in aspect. Still, if the primitive qualities of the planets (hot, cold, *etc.*) were in agreement, it would be a good testimony.

[152] *Gr. Intr.* VIII.4.1496*ff.*

benefaction from the services which he does, but even thanks will not be rendered to him because of them; and it will be possible that for the services which he does [provide], instead of money, blame will be brought to him, and from it he will get a malevolent attitude.[153] The same will happen to men in revolutions, if this Part and its Lord were disposed as was said.

The twelfth Part of the 11th house, which is called the Part of Necessity and the Love of Matters, according to the Persians, is taken in the day and night from Venus to the house of brothers; and it is projected from the Ascendant. Indeed according to the Egyptians, it is taken in the day [and night?] from Mars to the house of brothers, and is projected from the Ascendant.[154]

Chapter 15: On the Parts of the 12th house, and on their extraction and their significations

Mention must be made in this chapter of the Parts of the 12th house, and first on the Part of Hidden Enemies,[155] which is taken in the day and night from Saturn to Mars; and it is projected from the Ascendant.

The second Part of the 12th house, according to Hermes,[156] is taken in the day and night from the Lord of the house of enemies, to the degree of the house of enemies; and it is projected from the Ascendant.

And Abū Ma'shar said[157] that each of these Parts [above] ought to be used, [and] that if they were in the opposition or square aspect to their own Lords, or to the Lord of the Ascendant, the native or querent will have many enemies. If however they were both free from their Lord[s], and with the Lord of the Ascendant, he will not have enemies easily. The same will happen in revolutions, because if they were badly disposed, as was said, men will be inimical to each other in that revolution.

The third Part of the 12th house, which is called the Part of Labor and Affliction, is taken in the day and night from the Part of Things to Be to the Part of Fortune, and in the night the reverse; and it is projected from the Ascendant.

---

[153] *Acquiret inde malivolentiam.* Comparing this with Abū Ma'shar, it is clear he will ultimately get blamed; but it is unclear whether or not it will be in response to blaming he himself engages in. I believe the sense is that he will ultimately be the victim.

[154] But see below (the seventh and eighth Pars of the fifth section), where this Part is uses "Delay" (*dilationis*) instead of "Love" (*Dilectionis*). I am not sure why the 3rd is used here.

[155] Abū Ma'shar simply calls this the "Part of Enemies" (*Gr. Intr.* VIII.4.1510).

[156] As reported by Abū Ma'shar (*Gr. Intr.* VIII.4.1514), also called the "Part of Enemies" but without the "hidden" qualification.

[157] *Gr. Intr.* VIII.4.1516.

And Abū Ma'shar said[158] that this Part is like the Part of Mercury: which if it and its Lord were of good condition and well disposed, it signifies that the native or querent will be fortunate in his labors and will earn money from them, and they will be profitable for him. If however it were joined corporally with the Lord of the Ascendant without reception, or it were in his opposition or square aspect, he will be laborious for the whole time of his life; nor will his labors profit him, nor will he rejoice from his own goods, nor will he make money from them, nor will his fortune be profitable.

Chapter 16: On the recounting of certain Parts according to Abū Ma'shar, of which mention was not made above, which is called the "fifth section"[159]

In this chapter mention must be made of certain other Parts which were not distinctly listed above, which are ten Parts according to Abū Ma'shar,[160] which often occur in the work of the masters of this science when they want to judge on some nativity or general question, or some revolution.

Of which the first is called the Part of the *Hīlāj*,[161] and it is a matter which the ancient sages of this science very much observed, and they found it to be truthful. Which is taken (if it were a nativity, or question or conjunctional revolution) from the degree of the conjunction (indeed if it were preventional, from the degree of the prevention) both in the day and in the night to the Moon; and it is projected from the Ascendant.[162] And Abū Ma'shar said[163] that this Part is directed in the same way the *hīlāj* is directed. And if its direction (or profection) were to arrive at the benefics, it signifies good; indeed if it were to arrive at the malefics, it signifies evil and impediment, and danger to the native or querent, or to him for whom the revolution of the year is—or even if it were a universal revolution [of the years of the world]. And this is the reason why sometimes many honest men are deceived: because sometimes they see many contrary things devolve which ought not to devolve according to the *hīlāj*. For they considered only the *hīlāj*, [and] they do not care about the Part of the *Hīlāj*.

---

[158] *Gr. Intr.* VIII.4.1522-23.
[159] I.e., *Gr. Intr.* VIII.5 as a whole.
[160] *Gr. Intr.* VIII.5.1531.
[161] Recall that this Part was already listed under the Parts of the 1st house (Ch. 4 above).
[162] Bonatti's language makes it seem like the issue of a conjunctional/preventional chart only matters for a revolution, but he undoubtedly means this condition to apply to any kind of chart.
[163] *Gr. Intr.* VIII.5.1538.

You however should not neglect this, but always direct the Part of the *Hīlāj*, both in nativities and in questions and in revolutions, and you will not go astray. For it has its own peculiar significations apart from others, which are of great efficacy.

The second Part of the fifth section, which is called the Part of Lean Bodies, is taken in the day from the Part of Fortune to Mars, and in the night the reverse; and it is projected from the Ascendant.[164] And Abū Ma'shar said[165] if this Part were with the Lord of the Ascendant, or with a planet for which there is some dignity in the Ascendant or in the *al-kadukhadāh*, and the planet were in its own dignity or in a moist sign, the native will have great limbs. And he said if it were otherwise, and it were with Mercury or Mars, or these planets were to rule it, the native will be lean in body.

The third Part of the fifth section, which is called the Part of Warfare and Boldness, is taken in the day from Saturn to the Moon, and in the night the reverse; and it is projected from the Ascendant. And Abū Ma'shar said[166] this Part is like the Part of Reason and Profound Counsel[167] and the Part of the King and what Work the Native Will Do.[168] Which if it were in the sextile aspect of Mars or Jupiter in signs of animals, it signifies that the native will be bold, and a soldier, and a procurer of animals, and he will be a gladiator sporting with spears, arms, and swords.

The fourth Part of the fifth section, which is called the Part of Boldness and Strength and Rulership, is taken in the day from the Lord of the Ascendant to the Moon, and in the night the reverse; and is projected from the Ascendant. Which if it were in the sextile aspect of Mars or Jupiter, or [were] in the domiciles of the malefics, received, in strong signs, it signifies that its Lord[169] is spirited and strong in his body.

The fifth Part of the fifth section, which is called the Part of Cleverness and Skill and Sharpness and Learning (of all arts, and memory and the like), is taken in the day from Mercury to the Part of Things to Be, and in the night the reverse; and it is projected from the Ascendant. And wherefore the wise took this Part so, because all of these are signified by Mercury, and are attributed to him, and are rendered to the soul; and the Part of Things to Be signifies the

---

[164] This is identical to the Hermetic Lot of Mars (see above).
[165] *Gr. Intr.* VIII.5.1556*ff.*
[166] *Gr. Intr.* VIII.5.1564*ff.*
[167] The Part of Prayer and Profound Counsel, fourth Part of the 9th house above.
[168] See the eighth Part of the 10th house, above.
[169] This must refer to the native (or whoever is the subject of the chart).

condition [or nature] of the soul; and all of these proceed with the authority of the soul. Which if it were of good condition and well disposed, and were with Mercury in the nativity or question, and he were of good condition, it signifies the native will be clever with a good cleverness, of sharp skill, teachable, acting in many arts to learn everything he wishes, and in which he applies himself with less labor than others, and will retain well what he has learned, and all of these will profit him. But if they were made unfortunate and badly disposed, he will be fit to learn, but they will not be useful for him–rather he will find evil and something horrible because of the aforesaid. Indeed if Mercury were joined to Mars by a conjunction or aspect, and there were some testimony for Mars in the place in which the Part were to fall, it signifies the native or querent is going to be a robber and very keen thief, and that he will know how to open gates and bars on doors with craftiness and subtlety, without a key. If however it were a trine aspect or a sextile with reception, he will know how to do all things, but he will not do it in an evil way. The same will happen in revolutions, for if this Part were so disposed, as was said, the aforesaid will happen more in that revolution than they are used to happening in other times.

The sixth Part of the fifth section, which is called the Part of the Investigation of a Matter (and whether the matter will be generally perfected, or destroyed, or deferred, or brought forth to its effect), is taken in the day and night from Saturn to Mars; and it is projected from Mercury. This Part is extracted from these three planets because the malefics have signification over destruction. Which, even if sometimes they might impede by a square aspect or the opposition, still sometimes they perfect a matter (even if perhaps with slowness and duress); but the malefics, if they were to impede, destroy a matter; and if they did not destroy it, they will slow it down until hope is lost. And because Mercury participates in matters, therefore this Part is projected from him. Which if [the Part] were of good condition and well disposed, free from the malefics (namely from Mars in the day and Saturn in the night),[170] it signifies the effecting of the matter. And if it were impeded by one of them, as was said, it signifies its destruction, and it will not be perfected. And if it were perfected, it will not last. And Abū Ma'shar said[171] this Part is employed in unknown matters, and whose origin[172] is not known. If however it were a known matter,

---

[170] This is a sect matter–in diurnal charts, Mars will not operate as effectively and constructively; likewise for Saturn in nocturnal charts.

[171] *Gr. Intr.* VIII.5.1603*ff.*

[172] *Genus.* This could also mean "whose kind" is not known–i.e., since it is unknown we do not know how to classify it.

consider whether it would be either substance or marriage or any other matter: the matter will be looked at from its own place, and this Part will aid the significator signifying it.

The seventh Part of the fifth section, which is called the Part of Necessity and the Delay of Matters, is taken in the day and night (according to the Egyptians)[173] from Mars to the degree of the house of brothers, and it is projected from the Ascendant.[174] And this Part signifies the laziness and inertia of the native. Which if this Part were so disposed in a revolution,[175] it signifies that men will be such in that revolution.

The eighth Part of the fifth section, which ([like] the aforesaid) is called the Part of Necessity, and the Delay of Matters, is taken in the day and night (according to the Persians)[176] from the Part of Delay[177] to Mercury; and it is projected from the Ascendant.

And Abū Ma'shar said[178] each of these Parts is employed. Which if they were of good condition, and well disposed, it signifies the native will be half-concerned to carry through with his business affairs.[179] If however they were badly disposed, joined with malefics (or with one of them), or its Lord [were] with one of the malefics (and particularly with Saturn), or it and its Lord were with the Lord of the Ascendant, it signifies that the native will be lazy and inert, and will hardly be moved to do anything, and especially those things which are necessary for him [to do], unless perhaps by means of necessity forcing him [to do it].[180] Nor will he suddenly do something of those things which men do with the hope of usefulness; nor will his heart suffer to get involved in any merchant activities or other moneymaking matters, for fear he will lose [money] because of it; nor will he believe himself able, or know how, to make a living. And Abū Ma'shar said[181] if the Lord of this malefic were to impede the Lord of the house

---

[173] *Gr. Intr.* VIII.5.1608*ff.*

[174] Note the confusion between this and the alternative construction of the twelfth Part of the 11th house, the Part of Necessity and the Love of Matters. Probably "Delay" is the correct version here (due to Mars).

[175] See below for the instructions.

[176] *Gr. Intr.* VIII.5.1612*ff.*

[177] Reading *dilationis* for *dilectionis.*

[178] *Gr. Intr.* VIII.5.1614-15.

[179] But by this criterion, no one would ever be more than half-concerned to see things through. Abū Ma'shar leaves out the good conditions, so apparently Bonatti has filled them in. We should probably assume that a well-situated, fortunate Part (*etc.*) will allow the native to overcome sloth easily.

[180] Cf. also Tr. 9, Part 3, 10th House, Ch. 1, on determining whether a native will stick to one profession or make many shifts in his employment and interests.

[181] *Gr. Intr.* VIII.5.1620*ff.*

of substance, the native will destroy his own substance, and will not know how; or he will be harmed much in it, according to his condition [in life]. The same will happen in questions and in revolutions. For if the Part were just as was said, men in that year or revolution will be lazier and more fearful than usual.

The ninth Part of the fifth section, which is called the Part of Repayment, is taken in the day from Mars to the Sun, and in the night the reverse; and it will be projected from the Ascendant. Which if it were of good condition and well disposed in an angle (and especially in the 1st or 2nd) or in the succeedents of the angles (and especially in the 11th or 5th) with the Lord of the Ascendant in one of his own dignities, it signifies that the native will gladly repay those who have done well for him or who have exhibited some easily manageable service for him. If however it were of bad condition in the cadents from the angles (and especially in the 6th or 12th), nor [is it] with the Lord of the Ascendant nor [even] in one of his dignities, it signifies that he will receive something free from someone, nor will he repay well what was done for him. You may say the same in revolutions, if the Part were so located, because men will be observant in that revolution. You may understand the same in questions.

The tenth Part of the fifth section, which is called the Part of Truth and of Good Works, is taken in the day from Mercury to Mars, and in the night the reverse; and it is projected from the Ascendant. And Abū Ma'shar said[182] this Part is like the Part of Reason and Sense. Which if it were of good condition and well disposed, made fortunate and strong in an angle, it signifies that the native or querent will be observant of truth, and eager for good[183] works, and abhorring the contraries of these; and usefulness and success will happen to him because of this. If however this Part were impeded in an angle, he will exercise and observe truth, and good works, and harm and evil will come to him from that. And if it were outside the dignities of the Lord of the Ascendant, he will know good things but not exercise them. Which if it were so disposed in revolutions, men in those revolutions will be so disposed, and act accordingly.

And Abū Ma'shar said[184] these are the divulged Parts which the ancients described; and these are employed in nativities and in many places in revolutions of years and questions–namely each of of them in the places in which they are necessary. And he said, know that in many matters of the significations of the twelve houses and questions, and beginnings, and the revolutions of years, there

---

[182] *Gr. Intr.* VIII.5.1632.
[183] Reading *bonis* for *honis*.
[184] *Gr. Intr.* VIII.5.1639ff.

are Parts of which we have not made mention here. Because it is necessary with those Parts that we describe them in other books. And he said, however, what we have stated concerning the significations of the Parts in this book, are summaries in investigating, because the places of these Parts in the signs in which they are, and the conjunctions of the planets with them (or their aspects to them) change much of their significations for good or evil. And he said we will describe the investigation of their significations in their own places in the signs, in every book, in accordance with what is necessary.

Chapter 17: On the knowledge of certain extraordinary Parts about which mention was not made above

In this chapter we must look at certain extraordinary parts, about which mention was not made in the Parts of the seven planets, nor in the Parts of the twelve houses; nor in the recounting of the ten Parts of the fifth section. And these are very useful Parts, and in which one wanting to be intent on wealth can be more able to profit in revolutions.[185] For through these Parts you could weigh carefully the cheapness or dearness or mediocrity of the price of certain things born of the earth and of some other things for which it often is necessary that men have recourse to for their sustenance and for their necessities, like grain, wine, oil, and the like. You could even see whether there is going to be an abundance or scarcity of them. In the same way you could know why it should happen that a thing is sometimes abundant, and is expensive, and sometimes cheap. And sometimes it is not abundant, but rather there is little of it in quantity, and it is cheap; and sometimes it is expensive.

The aspects of the benefics to [a commodities-based Part] or to its Lord (not to mention to the Moon), or their corporal conjunction, signify its abundance; and the more so if the benefic who were to aspect the Part or its Lord of the Moon were the Lord of the domicile in which the Part were to fall. An aspect of the malefics to it, and the corporal conjunction, signifies a scarcity or need of them. You could examine the dearness or cheapness of a thing by the place of the Lord of the domicile or exaltation (or of the significator) in which [the Part] were to fall. Which if [that Lord] were in his own domicile or in his exaltation, or were otherwise made fortunate and strong, or were in an angle (and more seriously if he were in the 10th), it signifies the burdensomeness of the price of

---

[185] Reading *in revolutionibus* for *eam revolutionum*.

that thing. If however one were fortunate [and] the other unfortunate,[186] the condition of the thing will be changed little. But the Lord of the exaltation is less than the Lord of the domicile; however the Lord of the bound and the Lord of the triplicity adds or subtracts something. If however he were in the 12th in his own fall or his own descension, or in a cadent from the angle (and more strongly so if he were in the 12th or were combust), it signifies the cheapness and smallness of the price of the things. And [by] however much the significators were weaker, by that much more they signify the greater cheapness of the matter, and the smallness of the price. If however it were in one succeeding an angle (unless something else were to impede), it will neither be damaged much nor alleviated much. But if all the significators were fortunate, and strong, the matter will be burdensome, and will exceed measure in price; and more strongly so if they are in the 10th (as I said). Indeed if they were unfortunate and weak and badly disposed, they signify the ultimate cheapness of the thing and the smallness of its price.

And always let it be your concern to consider the matter of each of the significators, because every one of them gives and takes away according to its nature [or condition]. The significators are the Lord of the domicile, the exaltation, the Lord of the bound, the Lord of the triplicity; [those] of the planets from which the Part is extracted; and the planet which is the Lord of the domicile from which you begin to project the Part. However there is little power in the Lord of the face, so that one needn't be very concerned about it. However, the Lord of the domicile in which the Part were to fall, is to be preferred to the rest, and it must be judged more according to him, even though others add and subtract, just as was said–and the more strongly so, if he were of the planets from which the Part is extracted, because [the Part] will be much strengthened [in significance] by that.

Chapter 18: In which there is an example of the method of extracting some Parts

Now I will give you an example of one of the Parts for all of the other extraordinary Parts, and I will begin with the Part of Grain. Whence, if you wished to know the status of grain in some revolution, namely whether it will become cheaper or more expensive, or it may be had for a mediocre price, subtract the place of the Sun from the place of Mars, and add from above the degree and

---

[186] I.e., comparing the Lords of the domicile and the exaltation.

minute of the ascending sign, and project what was collected together from the beginning of the ascending sign, by giving 30° by equal degrees to each sign; and where the number were at an end, there will be the Part of Grain. Therefore you will consider the Lord of that sign, to see how it is disposed: because however much better he were disposed, grain will be that much more expensive, and however much he were more badly disposed, by that much more will it be cheap and worth less. You will even look at the other significators which I listed for you, to see how they are disposed: because those which were well disposed, will make for the increase of price and the scarcity of the thing; and those which were badly disposed, will make for the cheapness of the price and for its own abundance. And according to this you will judge of the rest (or of any other thing whose Part you seek), namely for every one in its own place and in its own condition [or nature], with the aforesaid aspects (and the Moon) being saved.[187] Which if the significator of the Part of Grain (or any other thing)–namely the Lord of the domicile in which it were to fall–were impeded, and of a bad condition and badly disposed, and if a benefic made fortunate and strong, and the Moon, were to aspect the Part, it signifies that grain (or whatever other thing whose Part you seek) will be in abundance and be cheap. If however a malefic were to aspect it, it will not be in abundance, but there will be little of it– however it will be cheap. And if its significator were made fortunate and strong, and well disposed, and a malefic were to aspect it, it signifies that grain (or whatever other thing whose Part you seek) will be expensive and rare. But if a benefic were to aspect him, it signifies that it will be in abundance (nevertheless however it will be expensive). You may understand this about all and every other individual Part.

On the Part of Barley[188]

If you wished to know whether barley is going to be cheap or expensive in the revolution which you seek, or what kind of status it will have, subtract the place of the Moon from the place of Jupiter, and add what remains by degrees and minutes of the ascending sign, and project from the Ascendant. And where

---

[187] *Salvis*, i.e., being sound or safe. This sounds awkward in this context. Perhaps this is merely an allusion to the Moon or the Parts being aspected by benefics, in good places in the chart, *etc.*

[188] In what follows I will compare Bonatti's list with al-Qabīsī's, pointing out where they differ. I also observe that Bonatti does not specify whether these Parts are to be changed in nocturnal figures–al-Bīrūnī says yes.

the number were ended, there will be the Part of Barley. You will judge according to the condition of the Lord of the sign by the aforesaid conditions.

On the Part of Beans[189]

If you wished to know whether or not beans are going to be cheap or expensive in the revolution which you seek, subtract the place of Saturn from the place of Mars, and add the degrees of the Ascendant to the remainder, and project from the Ascendant by giving 30° to every sign according to equal degrees, and where the number were ended, there will be the Part of Beans. Then you will judge as was said with the others.

On the Part of Onions[190]

You will find the Part of Onions and the Part of Green Peas in the same place [as above]; therefore it is not necessary for you to make another rule for them.

On the Part of Lentils

If you wished to know what the status of lentils will be, subtract the place of Mars from the place of Saturn, and add the degrees of the ascending sign to the remainder, and project from the Ascendant. And where the number will be ended, there will be the Part. You will judge according to it as was said with the others.

On the Part of Rice

You will take the Part of Rice from Jupiter to Saturn, and you will project from the Ascendant; and where the number were to fall, there will be the Part of Rice. You will judge of it as was said for the others.

On the Part of Sesame Seeds

The Part of Sesame Seeds is taken from Saturn to Jupiter, and is projected from the Ascendant; and it is a seed along the lines of flaxseed (but it is white) and doctors use it in certain antidotes.

---

[189] This is al-Qabīsī's lot of "Egyptian beans."
[190] Not in al-Qabīsī, but al-Bīrūnī lists the Lot of Beans and the Lot of Onions as being the same.

On the Part of Sugar[191]

The Part of Sugar is taken by subtracting the place of Mercury from the place of Venus, and add to what remains the degrees according to the ascending sign, and project from the Ascendant. And where the number will be ended, there will be the Part of Sugar, which you will consider as was said for the others.

On the Part of Dates

If you wished to know the market for dates, subtract the place of the Sun from the place of Venus, and add the degrees of the ascending sign to the remainder, and project from the Ascendant, and where the number were ended, there will be the Part.

On the Part of Honey

If however you wished to know the market for honey, subtract the place of the Moon from the place of the Sun, and add the degrees of the ascending sign to the remainder, and project from the Ascendant; and where the number were to end, there will be the Part.

On the Part of Wine[192]

Indeed if you wished to know the market for wine (which is had from the condition of the grapes), subtract the place of Saturn from the place of Venus, and add the degrees of the ascending sign to the remainder, and project from the Ascendant; and where the number were to arrive, there will be the Part which you seek. Judge on it as was said for the others.

On the Part of Olives

If it were your heart's desire to know whether there are going to be copious olives or not in the revolution which you seek, and you wished to know whether oil is going to be cheap or expensive, subtract the place of Mercury from the place of the Moon, and add the degree and minute of the ascending sign to the

---

[191] Not in al-Qabīsī, but al-Bīrūnī lists a Lot of Sugar as being calculated the opposite way: from Venus to Mercury, and projected from the Ascendant (and the reverse by night).
[192] Identical to al-Qabīsī's Lot of Grapes.

reminder, and project from the ascendant by giving 30° to each sign, by equal degrees; and where the number were ended, there will be the Part.

On the Part of Nuts[193]

If you wished to know whether or not there would be an abundance of nuts in that year or revolution, subtract the place of Mercury from the place of Mars, and add the degrees of the ascending sign to the remainder, and project this from the Ascendant; and where the number will be ended, there will be this Part—which you will judge as was said for the others.

On the Part of Silk and other Woven Things[194]

And if you wished to know the disposition of silk and its condition, and all other fine [small] things needing excessive dryness in life,[195] and of things loving temperate humidity, like millet, Italian panic-grass, melicgrass,[196] beans, and the like (even though silk does not like excessive humidity, though it is counted among these), it is taken in this way: namely, subtract the place of Mercury from the place of Venus, and add the degrees of the ascending sign to the remainder, and you will project from the Ascendant, so that where the number were ended, there will be this Part.

On the Part of Melons, Watermelons,[197] Cucumbers, and Gourds

In order to know whether there would be an abundance of melons, water-melons, cucumbers, and gourds, subtract the place of Mercury from the place of Saturn, and add the degrees of the ascending sign to the remainder; and where the number were ended, there will be the Part—regarding which you will judge just like the others.

---

[193] I do not find this in al-Qabīsī, and al-Bīrūnī's is calculated from Mars to Venus.
[194] *Coniunctorum.* Al-Bīrūnī calls this the "Lot of Raw Silk, Cotton."
[195] *Vita carentium nimia siccitate.* I take this to mean that cotton and silk need to be kept dry.
[196] *Melica.* This is a broad family of tall grasses that grow throughout the world. Bonatti is probably thinking of how strong grasses are woven together into baskets and such.
[197] *Citrullorum.* Zoller reads this as "lemons," which does pertain to the medieval *citrullus* as having to do with the color yellow. But as a vegetable, *citrullus* is a watermelon.

On the Part of Poisoned Things[198]

If you wished to know whether there would be a poisoning in that revolution or not, subtract the place of the Head of the Dragon from the place of Saturn, and add the degrees of the ascending sign to the remainder, and begin to project from the Ascendant. And where the number were ended, there will be this Part. You will judge regarding it as with the others.

On the Part of Wetness and Dryness[199]

In order to have the knowledge of the wet and the dry in the revolution, in the day subtract the place of the Moon from the place of Venus, and in the night the reverse, and add the degrees of the ascending sign to the remainder, and project from the Ascendant. And were the number were ended, there will be the Part which you seek. The judgment of it is as the others.

On the Part of Salted Things[200]

In order to know the market of salty things, through which you could understand the status of them and of salt (even if not perhaps to a fine degree, though to a useful one), subtract the place of Mars from the place of the Moon, and add the degrees of the ascending sign to the remainder, and project from the Ascendant. And where the number were ended, there will be this Part.

On the Part of Sweet Foods

In order to know the condition of sweet foods, subtract the place of the Sun from the place of Venus, and add the degrees of the ascending sign to the remainder, and project from the Ascendant]; and where the number were ended, there will be this Part.

---

[198] *Venenatorum.* This Part is identical to al-Qabīsī's Lot of Poisons, but the 1550 edition incorrectly reads *venatorum* ("hunters") missing the abbreviation mark (which inserts the extra *en*) in the 1491 edition–hence Zoller mistakenly translates this (with Bonatti) as the Part of Hunters. In Tr. 7, Part 2, 7th House, Ch. 12, Bonatti likewise treats this as the "Part of Hunting" in a section on hunting animals.

[199] I do not find this in either al-Qabīsī or al-Bīrūnī.

[200] This is al-Qabīsī's Lot of Purgative and Salty Medicines.

On the Part of Bitter Foods

In order to know the condition of bitter foods, subtract the place of Mercury from the place of Saturn, and add the degrees of the ascending sign to the remainder [and project from the Ascendant], and where the number were ended, there will be this Part.

On the Part of Acrid[201] Foods

In order to know the condition of acrid foods, subtract the place of Saturn from the place of Mars, and add the degrees of the ascending sign to the remainder, and project from the Ascendant; and where your number were ended, there will be this Part.

On the Part of Sharp[202] Foods

In order to know the condition of sharp foods and herbs having a sharp taste, subtract the place of Mars from the place of Saturn, and add the degrees of the ascending sign to the remainder, and project from the Ascendant.

On the Part of Sweet Medicines

In order to know the condition of sweet purgative medicines, subtract the place of the Sun from the place of the Moon, and add the degrees of the ascending sign to the remainder; and where the number were ended, there will be this Part.

On the Part of Acrid Medicines[203]

In order to know the condition of acrid medicines, subtract the place of Saturn from the place of Jupiter, and add the degrees of the ascending sign to the remainder, and project from the Ascendant. And where the number were ended, there will be this Part.

---

[201] *Acrium.* "sharp, pungent, hot, piercing." This is al-Qabīsī's Lot of Sour Foods (which in Latin would be *acerbus* or *acidus*). By the construction it seems this ought to pertain to pungent foods (due to its beginning from Saturn).

[202] *Acutorum.* This is al-Qabīsī's Lot of Pungent Foods (which would be *acer* as in the previous Part). But by the construction it seems this ought to pertain to sour foods.

[203] This is al-Qabīsī's Lot of Purgative and Sour Medicines.

On the Part of Salted Medicines

In order to know the condition of salted medicines, subtract the place of Mars from the place of the Moon, and add the degrees of the ascending sign to the remainder, and project this from the Ascendant. And where the number were ended, there will be the Part.

On the Part of the Disposition of the Year[204]

And there is another Part which seems to comprehend all of the aforesaid; and it seems that it is so correlated with them, and they with it, that it is generated from them, and that they are generated from it. And this is called the Part of Good Disposition, or of the Productiveness of the Year, which is taken from the Moon to Mercury, and is projected from the Ascendant; and where the number were ended, there will be this Part (the judgment of which is just like the others).

[A Hint on Extracting Longitudes]

Which if it were sometime to happen that a planet (whose place you want to extract from the place of another's), is in more signs and degrees and minutes than the other from which you must extract him, add twelve signs to the lesser one from which it is extracted. Afterwards you could extract what you wanted, and add the degrees and minutes of the ascending sign to the remainder, and project from the Ascendant by giving 30° by equal degrees to each sign; and where the number were ended, there will be the place. You will judge just as was said with the others.

On the regions where these will be

In order to know in which regions the aforesaid accidents will happen, you will consider from what direction the Lord of the Ascendant or of the 10th or 11th or the 4th is–whether in the eastern direction, or the southern or western, or northern; or in eastern signs (which are Aries and its triplicity) or southern (which are Taurus or its triplicity) or western (which are Gemini and its triplicity), or northern (which are Cancer and its triplicity).

---

[204] I am not sure what Bonatti's source for this Part is.

On the time [or season]²⁰⁵ when these will be

Indeed, to know the time [or season] in which the things signified by the aforesaid Parts ought to happen, and in what quarter [of the year] the signified thing will arrive, look at the Part which you wanted. Which if it were to fall in the Ascendant or between the Ascendant and the 4th, its signified thing will fall in the first quarter of that revolution of the year,²⁰⁶ or of that season in which the signified thing ought to happen.²⁰⁷ If however it were in the 4th or between the 4th and the 7th, it will happen in the second quarter. If indeed it were in the 7th or between the 7th and the 10th, it will happen in the third quarter. But if it were in the 10th or between the 10th and the Ascendant, it will happen in the last quarter of that time [or season]. And insofar as it is closer to the angle, it will happen faster; indeed, insofar as it is more removed from the angle, it will happen more slowly.

Chapter 19: On the number of the significators²⁰⁸ of any of the Parts

Every²⁰⁹ Part has at least two significators naturally, even though among those there are some which are sometimes content with only one: like the Part of Substance, if it were to fall in the 2nd; and likewise the Part of Journeys, if it were to fall in the 9th—[in which cases the Lord of that domicile is the significator].²¹⁰ And there are certain Parts which have three significators: the two from which the Part is extracted, and one from the domicile in which it were to fall (if

---

²⁰⁵ *Tempus* in Latin can mean "time" or "season"—as in English when we quote (or misquote) Ecclesiastes 3:1: "To everything there is a season; a time for every purpose under the Sun."
²⁰⁶ If we are judging from the Aries ingress.
²⁰⁷ I.e., if we are using a quarterly ingress.
²⁰⁸ By "significators" Bonatti generally means either (a) the planets whose locations are used in the extraction of the Part; and (b) the planets ruling the place of the Part or from where it is projected. The reason why some Parts have more significators than others, seems to be because planets might play multiple roles in some Parts. For instance, if a Part were extracted using Mars and Saturn, and the Ascendant from which the Part were projected were Scorpio, and the place of the Part itself were ruled by Saturn, then the Part would have only two significators. But if (in the same situation) the place of the Part itself were ruled by Jupiter, then the Part would have three sigificators (Mars, Saturn, Jupiter).
²⁰⁹ This section on the number of significators is based on *Gr. Intr.* VIII.8.
²¹⁰ Adding this clause in brackets based on *Gr. Intr.* VIII.8.2056-57. The idea is that if a Part falls in a house whose subject-matter is naturally signified by the Part, then the domicile Lord of that sign will be the sole significator, no matter what other planets were used in constructing the Part, or whoever was the Lord of the Ascendant or other point from which the Part was projected.

[the domicile] did not belong to the other two). And there are some Parts which have four significators: two from which the Part is extracted, and the third [ruling the place] to which it arrives; and the fourth one from which the projection begins.[211]

And a Part that it is satisfied with one significator is strengthened if its significator were to aspect it. Indeed a Part which has two significators is strengthened if each of its significators were to aspect it (and they give greater hope of perfecting what the Part intends–however the Lord of the domicile in which the Part were to fall, will be more worthy). Indeed if the Part were to have three significators, and two were to aspect it (indeed the third did not aspect it), there will not be so much strength of the Part in perfecting what the Part intended. But if only one were to aspect, and two did not aspect, its strength will be less again for its purpose. Indeed if none of them were to aspect, it will be less again, and what was done with the matter will come to be with burdens and duress in the revolution. You may say the same if the significators were saved according to their being delivered [from impediment]. But if they were impeded, you will speak according to their impediment. For if they were all impeded, what is signified by that Part will hardly or never appear. And if the significators were to aspect the Part by a praiseworthy aspect, he who had hope will see what he intended from it. If however they were to aspect with enmity, evil and contrariety will happen to him because of it.

It could be that no one of the planets having a role in the Part, aspects it; and another who naturally signifies what the Part signifies, aspects it–then something will happen from it, even though not wholly. Like if Jupiter (who naturally signifies substance) aspected the Part of Substance, nor did the other significators aspect it; or Venus aspected the Part of Marriage, nor did the other significators aspect it, it would signify some kind of effecting of the matter. Or [if] it were the knowledge of the Part of Slaves or Servants, and a significator did not aspect the Part, but Mercury (who naturally signifies slaves and servants) aspected it. But this will be less [in power] than what is signified by the significator of the Part; and this will be on the occasion of a certain person who introduces himself into the matter, perhaps unasked. And if the one aspecting the Part were to have some dignity in the domicile in which it[212] was, this will

---

[211] I.e., "the Lord of the place from which the projection begins."
[212] Contrasted with the following sentence, this seems to mean that the planet is in one of its own dignities; but the sentence *could* mean it has a dignity in the place in with the *Part* is.

happen from the direction[213] by which the one intending was hoping for, or from someone known to him. If however [the aspecting planet] were peregrine, he will not know whence this will happen to him. And if the planet aspecting the Part were made unfortunate, not receiving the Part, or it were impeded, there will be movements and rumors in it, and none of the thing (which the Part signified) is perfected.

And Abū Ma'shar said,[214] after this, look at the unfortunate [planet] to see if it is in an angle or one succeeding the angle, and were direct: the destruction or impediment will exist after it is thought to be perfected. Which if Saturn were the unfortunate one, the impediment will be [because of] someone of greater age. If indeed it were Jupiter, it will be because of religious men or judges and others coming in between them. Indeed if it were Mars, it will be because of some contention of his. Indeed if it were the Sun, it will be because of the king or the wealthy. But if it were Venus, it will be because of women. But if it were Mercury, and he were impeded, it will be because of some business matter. And if it were the Moon, and she were in increased light and number, she will be the reason that the matter is increased. And if she were in decreased light, she will be the reason that the matter is worsened and diminished.

[Additional Parts pertaining to kings and empires][215]

Al-Qabīsī said[216] that which is called the Part of the Kingdom and Empire, which is used in the revolution of years of the world, is taken from Mars to the Moon, and is projected from the Ascendant of the conjunction which signified the mutation of the kingdom.[217] You may understand the same in sects, because in a certain way [sects] are a ruling and rulership. Indeed according to others, it is taken from the degree of the Ascendant of the conjunction [to the degree of the Midheaven of the conjunction], and is projected from the degree of the Ascendant of the revolution. However, according to certain others, it is taken

---

[213] *Ex parte.* This does not mean "by primary directions," but by a topic–so that if it concerned friends, the matter will be perfected by friends.

[214] *Gr. Intr.* VIII.8.2129ff.

[215] The remainder of this Treatise is based on al-Qabīsī and Abū Ma'shar's *OGC*.

[216] See al-Qabīsī, V.17.

[217] This (and all of the variants mentioned in the remainder of the paragraph) is al-Qabīsī's "lot of rulership and authority." His source was Abū Ma'shar, who specifies that (a) the calculation should be reversed by night; and (b) this Part and its variants could also be used in all revolutions of the Saturn-Jupiter conjunctions (he does not say anything about being able to use it in every revolution of years of the world). He adds that the domicile ruler of the Part will show what kinds of idols the people will worship: fire for Mars, silver for Venus, *etc.*

from the degree of the Sun to the degree of the Midheaven of the revolution, and it is projected from the degree of Jupiter (and this opinion seems more fitting to me).

The Part of the Time of the Elevation of the King,[218] which signifies his lastingness, is taken at the hour of his elevation or introduction,[219] in the day from the Sun to the fifteenth degree of the sign of Leo, and is projected from the degree of the Moon; indeed in the night it is taken from the degree of the Moon up to the tenth degree of the sign of Cancer, and is projected from the degree of the Sun.

And there is another Part of the Kingdom or Empire, which is taken at the hour of his elevation,[220] in the day from Jupiter[221] to Saturn, and in the night the reverse; and it is projected from the Ascendant of the revolution of the year in which the king or Emperor is elevated (and anyone else is promoted to some lay dignity).[222] And al-Qabīsī said that if Jupiter were in a common sign, and the revolution were diurnal, and[223] Jupiter were cadent from the angles, it is taken from Saturn to Jupiter, and 30° are added; and it is projected from the Ascendant of the revolution of the year in which the king arose. Indeed if [Saturn and Jupiter] were opposed to each other, and were both cadent from the Ascendant, then half of the degrees which were between them is taken,[224] and it is projected from the Ascendant. Which if Jupiter were in Cancer and the revolution were nocturnal, this Part is taken from Jupiter to Saturn, and is projected from the Ascendant.

---

[218] This is al-Qabīsī's "lot of the duration of the rule," but several errors seem to have crept into the transmission of the doctrine. First, neither al-Qabīsī nor Abū Ma'shar make a diurnal-nocturnal distinction–Abū Ma'shar explicitly says to calculate both positions simultaneously. Second, Abū Ma'shar does not claim this Part pertains to the duration of the rule, but rather to the king's "nature." He wants us to see in whose domiciles these two positions land, and determine from them what the king will be engaged in: if they are in the domiciles of Saturn, he will be engaged in building and digging, *etc.*

[219] This could probably be used in conjunction with horary questions about kings' reigns–see Tr. 6, Part 2, 10th House.

[220] What puzzles me about this Part is that all of the considerations of Jupiter's and Saturn's placements seem to pertain to the revolution, not their condition on the day of the elevation to rule. I suspect that all of the considerations in this paragraph refer solely to the figure of the revolution of the year.

[221] Reading *Iove* for *Sole* (the Sun). Al-Qabīsī and Abū Ma'shar say "from Jupiter to Saturn."

[222] This is al-Qabīsī's "lot for the duration of the accession of the king," and Abū Ma'shar's "lot of the life span." Clearly Abū Ma'shar was envisioning that the king would remain in power until he died or was killed.

[223] Al-Qabīsī actually says "or," not "and," but Abū Ma'shar agrees with Bonatti (perhaps Bonatti's own edition of Abū Ma'shar said "and").

[224] In other words, the distance between them is divided in half.

Al-Qabīsī said[225] the first of the Parts by which the durability of the king[226] is examined, by means of his elevation, is that you look at the hour of the elevation of the kingdom, by which the projection of the year has arrived from the conjunction of the triplicity which signified the kingdom or sect, in terms of the number by which a year is given to every 30°, and one month to every 2° 30'. And when you have known in which sign or degree it was, save this; because that will be the place from which you will calculate the first Part. And when you wish to apply it,[227] you will determine[228] the Ascendant of the revolution of the year in which the king rose or was elected. After this, take [the distance] from the planet (either Saturn or Jupiter) oriental from the Sun in [the figure of the revolution of] that year up to the degree of the calculation of the first Part (which you have saved), and project from the Ascendant of the revolution. And where it reached, there will be the place of the first Part.

Indeed the second Part is that you look, in the month and day in which the king arose, from the [Saturn-Jupiter] conjunction in which the kingdom or empire arose, to see to what sign or what degree the profection of the year arrives (of the number by which a year is given to every 30°), and that is the place of the calculation of the second Part–save this, too. After this, take [the distance] from the planet occidental[229] from the Sun (namely from [either] Saturn or Jupiter), up to the place of the calculation of the second Part (which

---

[225] Abū Ma'shar's and al-Qabīsī's instructions for these two Parts are a bit clearer. First, we must calculate two profection points. We measure by profection (a) to what sign and degree the year has arrived from the mutation conjunction that shifted the Saturn-Jupiter conjunctions into the current triplicity (apparently from the date and zodiacal location of the conjunction itself); (b) to what sign and degree the year has arrived from the most recent Saturn-Jupiter conjunction. Then we look at the current revolution of the year in which the king has been elevated to the throne. In this chart, we measure the distance between either Saturn or Jupiter (whichever is oriental) to point (a), and project that from the Ascendant of the revolution in question. Then we measure the distance between either Saturn or Jupiter (whichever is occidental) to point (b), and project that from the Ascendant of the revolution in question. If they are both on the same side of the Sun, we use Saturn for the first Part and Jupiter for the second. Where the projections stop, are the locations of the Parts.

[226] Abū Ma'shar says these Parts indicate the king's life span.

[227] *Aptare.* I have translated this verb as "adapt" in Tr. 7, but I will translate it a bit more freely here so as to be in line with al-Qabīsī's own instructions.

[228] *Aptabis* (see above).

[229] Reading *occidentali* (following al-Qabīsī's and Abū Ma'shar's instructions) for Bonatti's *orientali.*

you have saved), and project it from the Ascendant of the revolution. And where it were to arrive, is the place of the second Part.[230]

These are Parts which signify the strength of the king and his durability.

---

[230] Bonatti omits to tell us how to delineate the Parts, presumably because he is following al-Qabīsī, who also omits them. Abū Ma'shar's instructions are interesting, but change the subject and ignore the Parts we have derived. He says we ought to count the degrees between the oriental (or occidental) planet and the Sun, multiply by 12, and divide by the number of degrees and minutes the oriental (or occidental) planet has traversed in its own sign. In the oriental case the result is how long the king will reign, giving a year to every 30°. In the occidental case, the result is added to the Ascendant, and one should count from the resulting degree to the degree of the oriental planet–those degrees will indicate how long the king will reign, giving a year to every 30°. As we can see, the whole profection procedure was in vain, so far as these instructions are concerned. But Abū Ma'shar says, in passing, that all of this is explained in greater detail in a book of his called the *Book of the Two Lots*. According to Yamamoto and Burnett, this book is otherwise unknown. See also my footnotes to Tr. 8, Part 1, Chs. 31 and 115.

BIBLIOGRAPHY

Abu Bakr, *Liber Genethliacus* (Nuremberg: Johannes Petreius, 1540)

Abū Ma'shar al-Balhi, *The Abbreviation of the Introduction to Astrology*, ed. and trans. Charles Burnett, K. Yamamoto, and Michio Yano (Leiden: E.J. Brill, 1994)

Abū Ma'shar al-Balhi, *Liber Introductorii Maioris ad Scientiam Iudiciorum Astrorum*, vols. VI, V, VI, IX, ed. Richard Lemay (Naples: Istituto Universitario Orientale, 1995)

Abū Ma'shar al-Balhi, *The Abbreviation of the Introduction to Astrology*, ed. and trans. Charles Burnett, annotated by Charles Burnett, G. Tobyn, G. Cornelius and V. Wells (ARHAT Publications, 1997)

Abū Ma'shar al-Balhi, *On Historical Astrology: The Book of Religions and Dynasties (On the Great Conjunctions)*, vols. I-II, eds. and trans. Keiji Yamamoto and Charles Burnett (Leiden: Brill, 2000)

Abū Ma'shar al-Balhi, *The Flowers of Abū Ma'shar*, trans. Benjamin Dykes (2nd ed., 2007)

Al-Biruni, Muhammad ibn Ahmad, *The Chronology of Ancient Nations*, trans. and ed. C. Edward Sachau (London: William H. Allen and Co., 1879)

Al-Biruni, Muhammad ibn Ahmad, *The Book of Instruction in the Elements of the Art of Astrology*, trans. R. Ramsay Wright (London: Luzac & Co., 1934)

Al-Fārābī, *De Ortu Scientiarum* (appearing as *"Alfarabi Über den Ursprung der Wissenschaften (De Ortu Scientiarum),"* ed. Clemens Baeumker, *Beiträge zur Geschichte der Philosophie des Mittelalters*, v. 19/3, 1916.

Al-Khayyat, Abu 'Ali, *The Judgments of Nativities*, trans. James H. Holden (Tempe, AZ: American Federation of Astrologers, Inc., 1988)

Al-Kindī, *The Forty Chapters (Iudicia Astrorum): The Two Latin Versions*, ed. Charles Burnett (London: The Warburg Institute, 1993)

Al-Mansur (attributed), *Capitula Almansoris*, ed. Plato of Tivoli (1136) (Basel: Johannes Hervagius, 1533)

Al-Qabīsī, *Isagoge*, trans. John of Spain, with commentary by John of Saxony (Paris: Simon Colinaeus, 1521)

Al-Qabīsī, *The Introduction to Astrology*, eds. Charles Burnett, Keiji Yamamoto, Michio Yano (London and Turin: The Warburg Institute, 2004)

Al-Rijāl, 'Ali, *In Iudiciis Astrorum* (Venice: Erhard Ratdolt, 1485)

Al-Rijāl, 'Ali, *Libri de Iudiciis Astrorum* (Basel: Henrichus Petrus, 1551)

Al-Tabarī, 'Umar, *De Nativitatibus* (Basel: Johannes Hervagius, 1533)

Al-Tabarī, 'Umar [Omar of Tiberias], *Three Books of Nativities*, ed. Robert Schmidt, trans. Robert Hand (Berkeley Springs, WV: The Golden Hind Press, 1997)

Alighieri, Dante, *Inferno*, trans. John Ciardi (New York, NY: Mentor, 1982)

Allen, Richard Hinckley, *Star Names: Their Lore and Meaning* (New York: Dover Publications Inc., 1963)

Aristotle, *The Complete Works of Aristotle* vols. I-II, ed. Jonathan Barnes (Princeton, NJ: Princeton University Press, 1984)

Bloch, Marc, *Feudal Society*, vols. I-II, trans. L.A. Manyon (Chicago: University of Chicago Press, 1961)

Bonatti, Guido, *Decem Tractatus Astronomiae* (Erhard Ratdolt: Venice, 1491)

Bonatti, Guido, *De Astronomia Tractatus X* (Basel, 1550)

Bonatti, Guido, *Liber Astronomiae: Books One, Two, and Three with Index*, trans. Robert Zoller and Robert Hand (Salisbury, Australia: Spica Publications, 1988)

Bonatti, Guido, *Liber Astronomiae Part IV: On Horary, First Part*, ed. Robert Schmidt, trans. Robert Hand (Berkeley Springs, WV: The Golden Hind Press, 1996)

Boncompagni, Baldassarre, *Della Vita e Della Opere di Guido Bonatti, Astrologo et Astronomo del Seculo Decimoterzo* (Rome: 1851)

Brady, Bernadette, *Brady's Book of Fixed Stars* (Boston: Weiser Books, 1998)

Burnett, Charles, ed., *Magic and Divination in the Middle Ages* (Aldershot, Great Britain: Ashgate Publishing Ltd., 1996)

Burnett, Charles and Gerrit Bos, *Scientific Weather Forecasting in the Middle Ages* (London and New York: Kegan Paul International, 2000)

Carmody, Francis, *Arabic Astronomical and Astrological Sciences in Latin Translation: A Critical Bibliography* (Berkeley and Los Angeles: University of California Press, 1956)

Carmody, Francis, *The Astronomical works of Thābit b. Qurra* (Berkeley and Los Angeles: University of California Press, 1960)

Dorotheus of Sidon, *Carmen Astrologicum*, trans. David Pingree (Abingdon, MD: The Astrology Center of America, 2005)

Grant, Edward, *Planets, Stars, and Orbs: The Medieval Cosmos, 1200–1687* (New York, NY: Cambridge University Press, 1994)

Haskins, Charles H., "Michael Scot and Frederick II," *Isis*, v. 4/2 (1921), pp. 250-75.

Haskins, Charles H., "Science at the Court of the Emperor Frederick II," *The American Historical Review*, v. 27/4 (1922), pp. 669-94.

Hermes Trismegistus, *Liber Hermetis*, ed. Robert Hand, trans. Robert Zoller (Salisbury, Australia: Spica Publications, 1998)

Holden, James H., *A History of Horoscopic Astrology* (Tempe, AZ: American Federation of Astrologers, Inc., 1996)

Ibn Labban, Kusyar, *Introduction to Astrology*, ed. and trans. Michio Yano (Tokyo: Institute for the Study of Languages and Cultures of Asia and Africa, 1997)

Ibn Sina (Avicenna), *The Canon of Medicine (al-Qanun fi'l tibb)*, ed. Laleh Bakhtiar (Great Books of the Islamic World, Inc., 1999)

Kennedy, Edward S., "The Sasanian Astronomical Handbook Zīj-I Shāh and the Astrological Doctrine of 'Transit' (Mamarr)," *Journal of the American Oriental Society*, v. 78/4 (1958), pp. 246-62.

Kunitzsch, Paul, "Mittelalterliche astronomisch-astrologische Glossare mit arabischen Fachausdrücken," *Bayerische Akademie der Wissenschaften Philosophisch-Historische Klasse*, 1977, v. 5

Kunitsch, Paul, trans. and ed., "Liber de Stellis Beibeniis," in *Hermetis Trismegisti: Astrologica et Divinatoria* (Turnhout: Brepols Publishers, 2001).

Kunitzsch, Paul and Tim Smart, *A Dictionary of Modern Star Names* (Cambridge, MA: New Track Media, 2006)

Latham, R.E., *Revised Medieval Latin Word-List from British and Irish Sources* (Oxford: Oxford University Press, 2004)

Lemay, Richard, *Abu Ma'shar and Latin Aristotelianism in the Twelfth Century* (Beirut: American University of Beirut, 1962)

Levy, Raphael, "A Note on the Latin Translators of Ibn Ezra," *Isis*, v. 37 nos. 3/4 (1947), pp. 153-55.

Lilly, William, *The Starry Messenger* (London: Company of Stationers and H. Blunden, 1652). Reprinted 2004 by Renaissance Astrology Facsimile Editions.

Lilly, William, *Anima Astrologiae*, trans. Henry Coley (London: B. Harris, 1676)

Lilly, William, *Christian Astrology*, vols. I-II, ed. David R. Roell (Abingdon, MD: Astrology Center of America, 2004)

Long, A.A. and D.N. Sedley, *The Hellenistic Philosophers*, vol. I (Cambridge: Cambridge University Press, 1987)

Māshā'allāh *et al.*, *Liber Novem Iudicum in Iudiciis Astrorum* [Book of the Nine Judges], ed. Peter Liechtenstein (Venice: 1509)

Māshā'allāh, *De Receptione* [*On Reception*] and *De Revolutione Annorum Mundi* and *De Interpraetationibus*, in *Messahalae Antiquissimi ac Laudatissimi Inter Arabes Astrologi, Libri Tres*, ed. Joachim Heller (Nuremberg: Joannes Montanus and Ulrich Neuber, 1549)

Māshā'allāh, *On Reception*, ed. and trans. Robert Hand (ARHAT Publications, 1998)

Maternus, Firmicus Julius, *Matheseos Libri VIII*, eds. W. Kroll and F. Skutsch (Stuttgard: Teubner, 1968)

Michelsen, Neil F., *The Koch Book of Tables* (San Diego: ACS Publications, Inc., 1985)

Mantello, F.A.C. and A.G. Rigg, eds., *Medieval Latin: An Introduction and Bibliographical Guide* (Washington, DC: The Catholic University of America Press, 1996)

New Oxford Annotated Bible, ed. Bruce M. Metzger and Roland E. Murphy (New York: Oxford University Press, 1994)

Pingree, David, "Astronomy and Astrology in India and Iran," *Isis* v. 54/2 (1963), pp. 229-46.

Pingree, David, "Classical and Byzantine Astrology in Sassanian Persia," *Dumbarton Oaks Papers*, v. 43 (1989), pp. 227-239.

Pingree, David, *From Astral Omens to Astrology: From Babylon to Bīkāner* (Rome: Istituto italiano per L'Africa e L'Oriente, 1997)

Pseudo-Ptolemy, *Centiloquium*, ed. Georgius Trapezuntius, in Bonatti (1550)

Ptolemy, Claudius, *Tetrabiblos* vols. 1, 2, 4, trans. Robert Schmidt, ed. Robert Hand (Berkeley Springs, WV: The Golden Hind Press, 1994-98)

Ptolemy, Claudius, *Tetrabiblos*, trans. F.E. Robbins (Cambridge and London: Harvard University Press, 1940)

Ptolemy, Claudius, *Quadripartitum* [Tetrabiblos], trans. Plato of Tivoli (1138) (Basel: Johannes Hervagius, 1533)

Sahl ibn Bishr, *Introductorium* and *Praecipua Iudicia* [The Fifty Judgments] *De Interrogationibus* and *De Electionibus*, in *Tetrabiblos*, ed. Girolamo Salio (Venice: Bonetus Locatellus, 1493)

Sahl ibn Bishr, *De Electionibus* (Venice: Peter of Liechtenstein, 1509)

Selby, Talbot R., "Filippo Villani and his Vita of Guido Bonatti," *Renaissance News*, v. 11/4 (1958), pp. 243-48.

Seneca, *The Stoic Philosophy of Seneca*, ed. and trans. Moses Hadas (New York: The Norton Library, 1968)

Stegemann, Viktor, *Dorotheos von Sidon und das Sogenannte* Introductorium *des Sahl ibn Bišr* (Prague: Orientalisches Institut in Prag, 1942)

Thomson, S. Harrison, "The Text of Grosseteste's *De Cometis*," *Isis* v. 19/1 (1933), pp. 19-25.

Thorndike, Lynn, *A History of Magic and Experimental Science* (New York: The Macmillan Company, 1929)

Thorndike, Lynn, *The* Sphere *of Sacrobosco and Its Commentators* (Chicago: The University of Chicago Press, 1949)

Thorndike, Lynn, "A Third Translation by Salio," *Speculum*, v. 32/1 (1957), pp. 116-117.

Thorndike, Lynn, "John of Seville," *Speculum*, v. 34/1 (1959), pp. 20-38.

Utley, Francis Lee (review), "*The Legend of the Wandering Jew* by George K. Anderson," *Modern Philology*, v. 66/2 (1968), pp. 188-193.

Valens, Vettius, *The Anthology*, vols. I-VII, ed. Robert Hand, trans. Robert Schmidt (Berkeley Springs, WV: The Golden Hind Press, 1993-2001)

Van Cleve, Thomas Curtis, *The Emperor Frederick II of Hohenstaufen: Immutator Mundi* (London: Oxford University Press, 1972)

Weinstock, Stefan, "Lunar Mansions and Early Calendars," *The Journal of Hellenic Studies*, v. 69 (1949), pp. 48-69.

Zoller, Robert, *The Arabic Parts in Astrology: A Lost Key to Prediction* (Rochester, VT: Inner Traditions International, 1989)

Zoller, Robert, *Bonatti on War* (2nd ed., 2000)

INDEX